The Inklings at Christmastide

By

William Murdock

*Remembering the Greatest
Gift of All...
Kindest Regards
WM*

TATE PUBLISHING
AND ENTERPRISES, LLC

Second Edition

The Inklings at Christmastime
Second Edition
Copyright © 2013 by William Murdock. All rights reserved.

No part of this publication may be reproduced, stored in a retrieval system or transmitted in any way by any means, electronic, mechanical, photocopy, recording or otherwise without the prior permission of the author except as provided by USA copyright law.

All scriptures referenced are from the *New International Version*.

Readings for Advent and Epiphany through the words of C.S Lewis, J.R.R.Tolkien, Joy Davidman, Dorothy Sayers, Charles Williams, those who inspired them and those they inspired.

The opinions expressed by the author are not necessarily those of Tate Publishing, LLC.

Published by Tate Publishing & Enterprises, LLC
127 E. Trade Center Terrace | Mustang, Oklahoma 73064 USA
1.888.361.9473 | www.tatepublishing.com

Tate Publishing is committed to excellence in the publishing industry. The company reflects the philosophy established by the founders, based on Psalm 68:11,
"The Lord gave the word and great was the company of those who published it."

Book design copyright © 2013 by Tate Publishing, LLC. All rights reserved.
Cover & interior design by William Murdock.

Published in the United States of America
ISBN: 978-1-62563-363-7
1. Biography & Autobiography / Literary
2. Religion / Devotional
13.04.16

The Inklings at Christmastide

Readings for Advent and Epiphany through the words of C.S Lewis, J.R.R.Tolkien, Joy Davidman, Dorothy Sayers, Charles Williams, those who inspired them and those they inspired.

By

William Murdock

Foreword By:

Dale Ahlquist

President of the American Chesterton Society

Second Edition

Dedication

For My Grandparents

To the Memories of the Best

Christmases of our Lives

Table of Contents

Foreword -1

Introduction -3

Advent -6

A Brief History of the Inklings -9

The Inklings and the Others -13

Daily Readings Through Advent - 41

Daily Readings Through Epiphany -101

Foreword

G.K. Chesterton says there are two ways of getting home, and one of them is to stay there. Most of us take the longer, more complicated route. And though all of our journeys are different, it is interesting how similar many of them are.

William Murdock discovered G.K. Chesterton because of the influence of two men, a writer and academic named Sheldon Vanauken and a Christian rock singer named Larry Norman. Interestingly enough, it was the same two men who first inspired me to read Chesterton. And in both cases, it was because of a connection with C.S. Lewis.

When I was in college in the 1970's, I spent a summer with my sister and her husband in southern California. One after- noon, I was reading Mere Christianity by C. S. Lewis. My brother-in-law saw me and asked, "So you like C.S. Lewis?"

"I love C.S. Lewis."
"Have you ever read G.K. Chesterton?" "I've never heard of G.K. Chesterton."

"If you like C.S. Lewis, you'll love Chesterton. In fact ..."

And then he said something that still drives people bananas when I repeat this story. "... If you read Chesterton, you don't need to read Lewis, because all of Lewis is in Chesterton."

I tucked away this blasphemous remark but did not forget it. The funny thing is I had never seen my brother-in-law read a book. He was a rock singer. His name was Larry Norman.

A few short years later I was preparing to get married to my wonderful wife Laura. I read Sheldon Vanauken's A Severe Mercy. The book contains many letters to the author from C.S. Lewis, and in one of them Lewis sings the praises of Chesterton's book The Everlasting Man as being one of the best works of Christian apologetics.

I took the hint and got my hands on The Everlasting Man and read it ... on my honeymoon. It was the beginning of not one, but two beautiful relationships. As I am now fond of saying, I've been married to my wife as long as I've been married to Chesterton.

Chesterton's influence on the Inklings is immeasurable. His wit and insight is delightful and profound, but there is more to him than his great quotations.

He has brought many of us the long way home: C.S. Lewis, Larry Norman, William Murdock, and many, many others. It is fitting that he forms an integral part of this book of readings on the Advent. He is always pointing the way to Christ, and like the Star of Bethlehem, he has led many wise men to the Truth.

Dale Ahlquist

President, American Chesterton Society

Introduction

This book actually started twenty some odd years ago when I began a correspondence with author Sheldon Vanauken after reading his book, A Severe Mercy. Having read a great deal of C.S. Lewis in a long search for a deeper realization of faith, I was drawn to the book by the simple fact that it mentioned Lewis on the cover. I had been raised Catholic and sought out God in other denominations, learning much about the scriptures and finding a great commonality amidst theological and parochial differences.

Being moved by the story of Van (as his friends called him) and his wife Davy, I learned that he was teaching history and literature at Lynchburg College in Virginia. With the audacity of youth and in hope of a response, I wrote to him telling what his book had meant to me and posed a few questions about his search for faith and how C.S. Lewis had played such a major part. Much to my surprise, he did answer and with that one small kindness, we embarked on a correspondence that lasted for years and helped illuminate the path on which I was stumbling.

The first letters were written on ten-cent postcards and addressed to me as William. After some time, he started addressing the cards to "Bill," and on the front of one of the cards, he inquired, "Is your given name actually Bill? I assumed it was William, and Bill was for intimate use." So Bill it was from then on as we continued our correspondence and friendship.

We would discuss his writings, as he would send copies of manuscripts he had written, copies of his books, and books written by others from whom he thought I would possibly benefit. The first time we spoke on the phone was on Christmas Eve in 1980. We talked about Advent, the meaning of the Christ Child, the incarnation, and the fact that his beloved Morgan had again broken down and was in the shop causing him to wait for friends to pick him up for dinner.

It was through his friendship and mentoring that I began to see the role that Christianity and Catholicism had in my belief as I looked for the light. That opened the world of the Inklings, their thought, and deep faith that has gone on to touch the lives of millions who had traveled the same course in which I found myself wandering.

But it was Chesterton that took me the rest of the way. And again, it came from a most unusual route. I had met an iconoclastic singer, songwriter named Larry Norman after a concert at Montreat-Anderson College in Montreat, North Carolina (home of the Reverend Billy Graham). I was impressed with the simplicity of his message, the straightforwardness of his lyrics, and the quiet joy that he radiated both on stage and as we spoke backstage after his performance.

During our conversation I had mentioned that something he had said on stage reminded me of something that C.S. Lewis had written, and he asked me if I had read much Lewis. I told him that I did. He then asked me if I had read anything by G.K. Chesterton. I told Larry that I had heard of him, but hadn't read any of his works. He told me that he had "found" Chesterton several years before while recording in England. "You should really read Orthodoxy and the Everlasting Man," he said. "If you like Lewis, I think you will love Chesterton."

I filed the conversation away in my mind but made sure that after that evening, I followed his career, listened to his albums, and read his articles, liner notes, and interviews. It was in one of these interviews that brought our conversation back to mind and that he mentioned his interest in G.K. Chesterton's writings and how they had influenced his thought and writing. He spoke of Chesterton's book Orthodoxy and how Chesterton's ideas "danced in his head." I took Larry's advice, read the book, and came all the way home.

Growing up, I loved Advent. It was my favorite time of year, and my grandparents filled the season with candles, nativity scenes, Advent wreaths, carols, high mass, and the reminder of the coming of the Savior. Somehow even though those weeks were filled with the hectic schedule of Christmas time, they seemed more peaceful than the rest of the year.

What you will find in the following pages is simply a collection of some of the most thoughtful, inspiring, and soul- searching works of the most intriguing men and women who have challenged the intellect and hearts of millions. Throughout countless decades they re-ask the eternal question that One asked two thousand years ago and resonates throughout history: "Who do you say that I am?

Merry Christmas.

William Murdock Advent, 2012

Asheville, N.C.

Chapter 1
ADVENT

The word Advent, taken form the Latin word adventus, simply means "coming." Since the year 900 AD, Advent has marked the beginning of the liturgical year. With the altars and vestments in penitent purple, it serves as a time of quiet reflection and prayer as we ready for the coming of the Savior, born in Bethlehem, to reconcile God and man. It is in this season that we prepare to celebrate Christ's Nativity. The Word of God made flesh to become the Lamb of God and to take away the sins of the world.

C.S. Lewis remarked that "Advent means 'coming'. What's coming in the reality of Christmas is an invasion. The world needs the invasion but doesn't want it. It's an invasion of human flesh and all creation by the Son of God; by the holiness of the creator Himself. This was not only an invasion, but also an all-out revolution.

Just when the tradition of observing Advent began is difficult to pinpoint. It certainly was not observed before the fourth century when the Feast of the Nativity was first established. Sermons from the fifth century reflect preparation for Christ Mass. But it was in the sixth century that Pope Gregory the Great (who held the Papal Throne from 1073-1085 and was the last monk to be elected Pope) formed Advent, as we know it today and whose writings include a homily for the second Sunday of Advent.

Advent begins the Sunday nearest to the feast of St. Andrew the Apostle (celebrated on the 30th of November) and continues for four Sundays, ending on Christmas. Advent may start as early as the 27th of November, giving Advent as many as 28 days or it may start as late as December 3rd, giving Advent only 21 days.

Because Christmas falls on a different day each year, the fourth week of Advent may not run the entire week. So even though there are 28 days of readings in this book, you may want to move on to the reading for Christmas Day on December 25th.

The reading for each day includes a morning and evening scripture reading, a quote from one of the Inklings or from one who inspired them or who they inspired, and a short thought on their wisdom.

May the peace of the new born Savior be with you this season as we hear the echoes of the words "O come, O come Emmanuel."

Chapter 2

A BRIEF HISTORY OF THE INKLINGS

In picking up this book, you may be asking yourself, "Who or what are the Inklings?" This is certainly a good question about a group with such an unusual name. For those of you who are familiar with the Inklings, you know that the only thing more unusual than the name is the group of men who comprised this amazing assemblage.

A group of friends who met twice weekly, the Inklings were comprised of some of the most renowned authors, writers, and thinkers of the 20th Century. During their informal meetings, they would discuss and critique each other's writing, converse about the events of the day, and any other subject that may have entered their astounding minds. Meeting from the early 1930s until late 1949, they met over tea, lunch, beer, dinner, and pipes, to read from their unfinished manuscripts, laugh, and at times, to see which one of them could read the worst prose they could find.

"Properly speaking," wrote Warren Lewis (a member of the Inklings and the older brother of C.S. Lewis), "the Inklings was neither a club nor a literary society, though it partook of the nature of both. There were no rules, officers, agendas, or formal elections."

This informal group of writers and thinkers would meet at Magdale College in the rooms of C.S. Lewis every Thursday evening or on occasion in the rooms of J.R.R. Tolkien at Oxford.

They would also casually meet on Tuesdays for lunch at noon at a local pub, the Eagle and the Child or as it was better known at Oxford, "The Bird and the Baby." In later years they would find themselves meeting at the Lamb and the Flag located across the street. But no matter where they met, "The Bird" would always be considered home.

The Inklings drew their name from a club at University College, of which both Tolkien and C.S. Lewis were members. The original Inklings, which began in 1931, was formed to give an opportunity for students and instructors to present their compositions that were yet unfinished. In 1933, the club waned and it was then that Lewis and Tolkien re-established the group at Magdalen College.

Tolkien would muse about the club's name as "a pleasantly ingenious pun in its way, suggesting people with vague or half-formed intimations and ideas, plus those who dabble in ink." It was there that some of the world's most beloved fantasies and theological allegories was first read and heard.

It was the Inklings that first listened to and discussed the initial drafts of C.S. Lewis' The Great Divorce, Out of the Silent Planet, and the Narnia stories (which Tolkien didn't care for, citing them too simplistic), Warren Lewis' biography of Louis XIV, Tolkien's The Hobbit and The Lord of the Rings, and Charles Williams' All Hallows' Eve, among many others.

The Thursday evening meetings, which would also include their usual ham supper, were where they would read their works, and Tuesday lunches were where more informal discussions were held. They would usually begin with Lewis asking one of the members to read from a manuscript on which they were working.

After the reading, the group would then discuss what had been read and freely critique what they had heard. "We were no mutual admiration society: praise for good work was unstinted, but censure for bad work or even not-so-good work, was often brutally frank. To read to the Inklings was a formidable ordeal," commented Warren Lewis on what the Inklings were like.

The Inklings, as with most literary groups at Oxford at the time, were comprised of all men. The membership of the Inklings, albeit informal, included authors: J.R.R. Tolkien, C.S. Lewis, Charles Williams, Warren Lewis, Adam Fox, E.R. Eddison, and Owen Barfield; professors: J.A.W. Bennett, Lord David Cecil, C.E. Stevens, Nevell Coghill, Colin Hardie,

Charles Wrenn, R.B. McCullum; physician R.E. Harvard; and lecturers: Gervase Matthew, Hugo Dyson, Christopher Tolkien (J.R.R. Tolkien's son), and John Wain. It is important to note that not all members attended all meetings or remained as long as others.

But it was the core of Lewis, Tolkien, Williams, Barfield, and a few others that kept the group together. But no matter who was in attendance, they enjoyed their meetings, friendships, and each other's company immensely. This was evident in C.S. Lewis' comment on the Inklings meetings:

"Our fun is often so fast and furious that the company probably thinks we are talking bawdy, when in fact, we are very likely talking theology."

The Inklings ended as they started, almost out of nowhere. In fact, one Thursday night in October, no one turned up. The last Inklings meeting was held on October 20, 1949, with its traditional ham supper. It was noted in Warren Lewis's diary on the next Thursday that "no one turned up after dinner, which was just as well as Jack had a bad cold and wanted to go to bed early." The next week, Warren wrote in his diary, "No Inklings tonight, so dined at home." The Inklings were not mentioned in his diary again.

Even though the Thursday evening Inklings meetings had abruptly ended, the Tuesday luncheon meetings at mid-day (now moved to Monday to fit the members' schedules better) continued at the "Bird and the Baby" until Lewis's death in 1963. It was Inkling member John Wain, author and professor at Oxford, who probably eulogized the group best, "The best of them were as good as anything I shall live to see."

Chapter 3

THE INKLINGS AND THE OTHERS

G.K. CHESTERTON

G.K. Chesterton (1874-1936)

George Bernard Shaw called him a "Man of Colossal Genius," and Gilbert Keith Chesterton was certainly that. Born in London on May 28th, 1874, Chesterton didn't speak until he was three years old, and didn't learn to read until he was eight. Even so he was always drawing pictures, showing even then the fierce and creative mind that the world would one day embrace. His life-long love of fairy tales, poetry, and fiction began during these early years.

Influenced predominantly by George MacDonald and his The Princess and the Goblin, Chesterton commented that he "made a difference to my whole existence and helped me see things in a different way from the start." The story, he said, brought him to see all ordinary staircases and windows into magical things and even more importantly brought him to the realization that "when evil things besieging us do appear, they do not appear outside but inside."

At the age 13, he entered what was at the time the equivalent of high school, but never attended college, save for a few classes and never received a degree. Chesterton began his journalistic career in 1896 working for the London publisher Redway and T. Fisher Unwin. Trained initially as an illustrator, Chesterton was approached in 1900 to write a number of articles on art criticism, and thus the artist became the writer.

He married his love, Francis Blogg in 1901. The next year he was assigned to write a weekly column in the Daily News, and three years later was approached by London's leading newspaper The Illustrated London News to move his column, where his fame and popularity spread and he worked for the next 30 years.

He wrote on theology, politics, travel, history, poetry, social issues, economics, children's stories, and mysteries. He authored nearly 100 books, 200 short stories (including the widely popular Father Brown Mysteries), 4,000 essays, thousands of newspaper articles, wrote articles for the Encyclopedia Britannica, and wrote and published his own weekly newspaper simply named GK's Weekly. The little boy who did not read until he was eight had become one of the most prolific writers in history.

Converting to Catholicism in 1922, Chesterton quickly became the most well-known and heeded apologist of his time (one could easily argue of all time). Weighing 300 pounds and standing 6'4", he was an impressive figure with his rumpled hat, cape, and ever-present sword-stick (sometimes accompanied with a knife and loaded revolver). Chesterton carried these things not as protection but as an extension of his imaginative thinking, and I am sure hoping that he would be caught up in some great adventure in which these items would come in quite handy in defending himself. A close friend once commented on Chesterton's appearance as "...a walking blasphemy, a blend of the angel and the ape."

In a famous spirited exchange with friend and author George Bernard Shaw, who himself was quite thin; Chesterton noted "to look at you, anyone would think there was a famine in England." Shaw promptly retorted, "To look at you, anyone would think you caused it." All who knew him or even knew about him at the time would be quick to attest that the only thing larger than his physical appearance was his intellect.

As much as he enjoyed writing, he enjoyed debating just as much. He gleefully took on some of the greatest minds of his era in friendly but spirited debates. He traded wits and philosophies with H.G. Wells, Clarence Darrow, Bertrand Russell, and his old friend and "friendly enemy" George Bernard Shaw. Always quick to laugh at himself, he brought serious humor and deeply searched thought to what would lead countless men and women to the love and understanding of orthodoxy. Chesterton passed away on June 14th, 1936, in Beaconsfield, Buckinghamshire, at the age of 62

JOY
DAVIDMAN

Joy Davidman (1915-1960)

The beloved wife of C.S. Lewis, Joy Davidman was born in New York City on April 18th, 1915. The daughter of Jewish immigrants, Joy grew up in a home that was steeped in the importance of education and was surrounded by books on philosophy, literature, and history. Entering Hunter College at the age of 15, Joy earned her Master's degree from Columbia at the age of 19.

Witnessing firsthand the devastation of the Great Depression in America during the 1930s (including seeing a orphan who had been fighting hunger commit suicide by jumping from the roof of a building on the Hunter College Campus) and the apparent shortcomings of the American Economic System, Joy turned to a Marxist philosophy that strongly influenced her writings for the next two decades. Joy joined the Communist Party in 1938 and published her first book of poetry that year, "Letter to a Comrade," for which she received the prestigious Yale Younger Poets Award, sharing the honor with poet Robert Frost.

Her writing career continued as she wrote for the Communist Publication, The New Masses, worked for MGM as a screen writer, and published Anya, her first novel and other editions of her poetry, including Seven Poets in Search of an Answer, War Poems of the United Nations, and her second novel, Weeping Bay.

In 1942, Joy married William Gresham and had two sons, David and Douglas. The marriage was troubled nearly from the start and ended in divorce. It was during this time that she began reading the works of C.S. Lewis, which precipitated her conversion from communism to Christianity.

In 1954, she wrote her first book reflecting her new faith titled Smoke on the Mountain, an Interpretation of the Ten Commandments in Terms of Today. She began a correspondence with Lewis, eventually moved to England where they met, became friends, fell in love, and married in 1956.

Joy Davidman succumbed to bone cancer and died on July 13th, 1960 in England, with her much loved Jack (C.S. Lewis) at her side.

C.S. LEWIS

C.S. Lewis (1898-1963)

Clive Staples Lewis, or Jack as his friends knew him, was born in Belfast, Ireland, on November 29, 1898, to a Welsh solicitor and the daughter of an Anglican priest. In a little more than six decades he would inspire faith and fuel the imagination of all readers who were to follow.

Lewis abandoned his Christian faith at the age of 15, declaring himself an atheist. He saw religion as more of a drudgery and obligation than a heart-felt closeness with God. Although he closed the door to religion, Lewis never seemed to stop searching for the truth and as a young man expressed his anger at God for not existing.

Educated at Oxford, his relentless intellect brought him to the volumes of George MacDonald, which took him from atheism to theism in 1929. But his search for the truth did not end there. It was thanks to his close friendship with fellow Oxford instructor J.R.R. Tolkien and reading G.K. Chesterton's The Everlasting Man that Jack was again convinced that Jesus Christ was the Son of God.

Considering himself "the most reluctant convert in all of England," Lewis would write dozens of books on literature (Studies in Words, An Experiment in Criticism, and The Discarded Image), theology (including The Abolition of Man, The Screwtape Letters, Mere Christianity, Miracles, and The Problem of Pain), children's stories (The Chronicles of Narnia), science fiction (Out of the Silent Planet, Perelandra, and That Hideous Strength), poetry (Spirits in Bondage, and Dymer) and fiction (Until We Have Faces, The Great Divorce, and The Pilgrim's Regress).

Lewis married Joy Davidman in 1956 and, following her death in 1960, wrote of his struggle with faith in the wake of losing his dearly loved wife. He died of renal failure one week before his 65th birthday.

Lewis passed away at home on November 22, 1963, the same day in which President John F. Kennedy was assassinated, and that A Brave New World author Aldous Huxley died.

The legacy left by C.S. Lewis has transcended literature and faith more than any other writer of the 20th century. From Narnia to Perelandra, the story of man's fall and redemption through God's love and Jesus' sacrifice is magnified on every page. He has touched the hearts of readers everywhere in search for the truth.

GEORGE MACDONALD

George MacDonald (1824-1905)

C.S. Lewis said of George MacDonald, "I know hardly any other writer who seems to be closer, or more continually close to the Spirit of Christ Himself."

MacDonald was born on December 10, 1824, in Huntly, Scotland, to a humble farmer and his wife in the midst of a hardscrabble existence. He grew up in the Calvinist dogma, but rejected the teachings of predestination, believing that God's love is open to all, and not just a select few. This theology permeated his thoughts, sermons, and writings. Beginning his ministry as the pastor of Trinity Congregational Church in 1850, MacDonald's teaching of the vastness of God's love was far from well received, and he spent much of his ministry life moving from position to position including a stint as an instructor at the University of London.

His life was far from easy as he and his family battled tuberculosis, abject poverty, and continual attacks on his teachings. It was through his writings that he found his voice and medium that had eluded him at the pulpit. His fantasy stories, At the Back of the North Wind, Lilith, Phantastes, Sir Gibbie, and The Princess and the Goblin, along with his fairy tales, The Golden Key and The Light Princess, along with his theological writings, which include Getting to Know Jesus, The Miracles of Our Lord, Unspoken Sermons, and Life Essential, brought him international recognition.

This acknowledgment opened the door to forging friendships with the most influential literary names of his era including Charles Dickens, Alfred Lord Tennyson, Mark Twain, Henry Longfellow, Walt Whitman, and Lewis Carroll (who he advised and persuaded to put his novel Alice in Wonderland up for publication).

In the anthology of MacDonald's writings, in which he served as editor, C.S. Lewis again remarked, "In making this collection, I was discharging a debt of justice. I have never concealed the fact that I regarded him as my master; indeed, I fancy I have never written a book in which I did not quote from him. But it has not seemed to me that those who have received my books kindly take even now sufficient notice of the affiliation. Honesty drives me to emphasize it."

MacDonald died after a long illness on September 18, 1905, at his home in Surry, England, at the age of 80

LARRY NORMAN

Larry Norman (1947-2008)

Heralded by the New York Times as "Christian Rock Music's most intelligent writer and greatest asset" and by Time Magazine as "probably the top solo artist in his field" and "the father of Jesus Rock," Larry Norman was born in Corpus Christi, Texas, on April 8, 1947, the son of a high-school English teacher and a homemaker. Upon moving to the Haight-Ashbury district in San Francisco in 1950, Larry began singing and playing the piano by age four and writing and performing his own songs by the age of nine.

Forming the band People! Larry opened for the largest names in the music industry of the day, including Janis Joplin, Jimi Hendrix, and the Doors. People! had a top ten hit in 1968 with a cover of the Zombies hit song I Love You. The day the album was released, Larry left the group to pursue a solo career, launching what is considered to be the first Christian Rock album in 1969, Upon This Rock.

Larry wrote and recorded what is thought by many to be the most significant and influential Christian album of all time in 1972. Only Visiting This Planet (produced by Beatles producer George Martin) featured a number of his most powerful songs, including Why Should the Devil Have All The Good Music, Why Don't You Look Into Jesus, and I Wish We'd All Been Ready.

His songs spanned all aspects of this life focusing on faith, politics, love, despair, and social conditions. He followed Only Visiting This Planet with So Long Ago the Garden, and In Another Land, giving Christian Rock and possibly all rock and roll its first trilogy.

Founding his own record label, Solid Rock Records, in the 1970s, Larry recorded nearly 100 albums and produced and guided the early careers of friend and collaborator Randy Stonehill, Mark Heard, Daniel Amos, Salvation Air Force, and Tom Howard. Throughout the years, more than 300 artists recorded Larry's songs including Petula Clark, Cliff Richards, and Sammy Davis Jr.

Always the innovator, in 1981 Larry founded Phydeaux Records to produce and distribute his catalog of music and that of other artists he produced. His music was far from being confined to albums and compact discs. His live performances drew capacity crowds as he performed and headlined at the London Palladium, the Hollywood Bowl, the White House, sold out the celebrated Royal Albert Hall in London six times, and opened the Sydney Opera House. He was inducted into the Gospel Music Hall of Fame in 2001 along with Elvis Presley.

Often misunderstood with his blond hair reaching well beyond his shoulders and his outspoken and unyielding message of God's love and Jesus' sacrifice to bring us back to the father, Larry shone the light of God's Son to darkened corners of a generation that had lost its way.

He brought countless souls back to God by the unique way he framed the unchanging message of Jesus' redemption and still does today. Larry Norman passed away from heart failure on February 24, 2008, at the age of sixty in Salem, Oregon.

DOROTHY SAYERS

Dorothy Sayers (1893-1957)

Born to a clergyman and his wife in Oxford, England, on June 13, 1893, Dorothy Leigh Sayers began learning Latin from her father at age six. At age 15, Somerville College at Oxford awarded her a scholarship where she received "first-class honors" after only a year of study. Even though she mastered her course of study, she was not awarded a degree, as women were not granted degrees during that time. But as times changed, Dorothy was one of the first women in England to receive a degree, thus helping to open the doors of education to women everywhere.

Dorothy's writing career certainly followed an unusual path. Her first book was published in 1916 and for the next few years Dorothy worked for her publisher as a teacher throughout France and Normandy as the Great War began. It was from there that her writing skills grew in a most unusual venue for the woman who would become one of the most popular poets, novelists, essayists, and Christian writers of any generation; she became a copywriter at one of the largest advertising agencies in London. It was there she created the famous Guinness "Zoo ads" and she is also believed to have coined the phrase, "It pays to advertise."

Best known for her fictional detective stories, Dorothy created the popular sleuth Lord Peter Wimsey, who kept readers guessing throughout a dozen novels and short stories. Her writing was far from contained on the advertising sideboards and mystery stories. She wrote widely on the war, woman's education, the ethics of advertising, and other subjects that kept her readers turning the page.

Her Christian faith and beliefs are an evident thread through many of her detective stories such as The Nine Tailors. A great admirer of G.K. Chesterton, Dorothy enjoyed friendships with C.S. Lewis, Charles Williams, and T.S. Eliot.

Her most well known theological writing can be found in the book The Mind of the Maker, which is an analogy that explores the Blessed Trinity, through her Anglican eyes and heart. As with many writers, her time was spent on the page many times until dawn. In her later years, she was fascinated by the stage and wrote several plays and turned her talents to translating the classics from the original language, the most notable being Dante's Divine Comedy and The Song of Roland.

Dorothy married Scottish journalist Arthur Fleming in 1926 and remained married until his death in 1950. She continued to write and enthrall readers until her untimely death at her Sunnyside Cottage, in Witham, Essex, of a stroke on December 17, 1957. Dorothy was 64 years old.

J.R.R TOLKIEN

J.R.R. Tolkien (1892-1973)

The man who would be known across the world and the generations as "the master of middle-earth" was born on January 3, 1892 christened John Roland Reuel Tolkien, and he was the first-born son of a British banker and his wife. While most of Tolkien's readers believed he was born in England, South Africa was actually the land of his birth due to his father being promoted to head his company's Bloemfontein office in an attempt to control widespread fraud in the burgeoning diamond trade.

At the age of three, Tolkien returned to England with his mother and younger brother, Hilary, to await his father's return. But shortly after their arrival, his father passed away from rheumatic fever before he was able to rejoin his family. Knowing the importance of education and now being without a husband or income, she began home schooling her two sons.

It was during this time that Roland (as he was called) began to be fascinated by languages, studying Greek, Latin, Welsh, English, and creating languages of his own. His mother, Mabel, converted to Catholicism, much to the dismay of her family, who quickly cut her off from the family's finances.

Struggling to raise and educate her two boys, she developed diabetes and passed away four years later at the age of 34. Roland and Hilary were left in the care of Father Francis Morgan at the John Henry Cardinal Newman's Oratory and attended the King Edward's School in Birmingham.

In 1916, Tolkien married Edith Bratt, eventually having four children. Graduating Exeter College at Oxford, he joined the signal corps, one of the most decorated units in the war. It was there in the trenches of France that he conceived the concept of Middle-Earth.

It was said that seeing the ravages of war, Tolkien didn't care for the age in which he was living so he created his own. It was during this time he began his writing in earnest.

After the war, Tolkien worked for the Oxford English Dictionary and also worked as a reader of the English language at the University of Leeds. He returned to Pembroke College at Oxford as a professor of the Anglo-Saxon language. It was there that he wrote The Hobbit, bringing Bilbo Baggins, Frodo, and Gandalf to life.

Upon publishing The Hobbit in 1937, Tolkien began writing The Lord of the Rings trilogy, a sequel to The Hobbit. The Lord of the Rings, The Two Towers, and The Return of the King were published nearly twenty years after The Hobbit brought us into Middle-Earth.

A devout Catholic, influenced by Saint Thomas Aquinas and G.K. Chesterton, Tolkien cited their works and influence and always stated that the "Lord of the Rings was a fundamentally religious and Catholic work."

His writing far from ended with the Hobbit tales. Tolkien was one of the most prolific writers of his age, writing more than fifty books and short stories.

Tolkien was a founding member of the Inklings. The first drafts of The Lord of the Rings and Lewis' The Great Divorce were first heard, discussed and critiqued during their twice-weekly meetings.

Tolkien spent his waning days avoiding, to the best of his ability, the celebrity that his stories and characters bestowed on him, returning to his earlier writing. The father of epic fantasy passed away in Bournemouth, England from pneumonia on September 2, 1973, at the age of 81.

SHELDON VANAUKEN

Sheldon Vanauken (1914-1996)

Born in Carmel, Indiana, on the day that England declared war on Germany, August 4th, 1914, Sheldon Vanauken would be best known to the world for chronicling his life and conversion in the best-selling book, A Severe Mercy in 1977.

The older of two sons born to prominent attorney Glenn Vanauken and his wife Grace, Van grew up in Indiana on his parents' estate christened Glenmerle. He began his early education attending military academies and earning his undergraduate degree from Wabash College, a small, private college for men in Indiana, and continued his studies at Yale and Oxford.

It was at Wabash College that Van met Jean Davis, or Davy, as she was known to everyone. Shortly after meeting, Van and Davy fell in love and pledged to each other a "Shining Barrier" that would protect their love against any and everything that might try to prevail against their affection for each other. They were the center of each other's universe.

In the fall of 1937, less than a year after they met, they secretly married. As World War II loomed, Van joined the Navy and was stationed in Hawaii, along with Davy. He was there on December 7th, 1941, and witnessed from a hillside overlooking the Pacific Fleet, as the Japanese attacked the United States and thrust the United States into war with Japan. With the end of the war, Davy and Van returned briefly to Glenmerle, and there built a sailing sloop named the Grey Goose (after the bird that has only one mate for life). They sailed together for some time through the Caribbean, the Chesapeake Bay, and the Florida Keys.

Taking a sabbatical from teaching history at Lynchburg College, he and Davy traveled to Oxford, and found themselves welcomed by a group of Christian students (Van and Davy being agnostics at the time) and became fast friends with one of Van's literature instructors, who was also a Christian, named C.S. Lewis.

It was Davy who first became a Christian, and fearing a breach in the "Shining Barrier," a hesitant Vanauken followed her into her newfound faith. Returning from England, Van returned to his teaching position at Lynchburg College. In the summer of 1954, Davy was diagnosed with a liver ailment, believed to have been contracted during their time at sea. She passed away less than a year later in January of 1955.

Twenty-two years later, Van told their poignant story of the "Shining Barrier," and how their love was, in Vanauken's words, "invaded by Christ." His love for Davy never waned and he never married again.

Van continued teaching at Lynchburg College and writing books, including Under the Mercy, Gateway to Heaven, Mercies: Collected Poems, The Glittering Illusion, and Little Lost Marion. Vanauken converted to Catholicism from Anglicanism in 1981 and wrote a number of articles and essays reflecting his Catholic faith, history and literature. He lived his life, as he signed off in his letters, "Under the Mercy."

Sheldon Vanauken died on October 28, 1996, at Lynchburg Hospital, just a few weeks after being diagnosed with cancer. He was 82 years old. His ashes were scattered in the churchyard of St. Stephen's Episcopal Church, as was Davy's four decades before; the "Shining Barrier" never broken.

CHARLES WILLIAMS

Charles Williams (1886-1945)

One of the lesser-known members of the Inklings, Charles Walter Stansby Williams held no less the stature and admiration of his fellow writers and readers worldwide. Born in London in 1886, the only son (he had a younger sister, Edith, three years his junior) of Richard Williams and his wife Mary, Charles was educated at the St. Albans School where he won a Junior County Scholarship. Upon graduation, Williams was granted a scholarship to University College London. He married Florence Conway in 1917, and they had one son.

Even though Williams' scholarship was exemplary, he was forced to abandon his studies and the University due to lack of funds. For four years he worked in the Methodist New Connexion Bookroom, and in 1908, he was hired by Oxford University Press as a proofreading assistant and quickly became an editor (editing the first English Language edition of the works of Søren Kierkegaard). He remained in their employ, holding numerous positions until his death in 1945.

Although he was well known and respected as a proofreader, editor, and literary advisor, it was his passion and talent for writing that would eventually gain him recognition. He published his first book of poetry The Silver Stair in 1917 and remained true to the page for more than 30 years. During those three decades, he lectured and wrote more than 30 books running the gamut from plays, fiction, and verse to literary criticism, biographies, and theology.

His importance as a writer and member of the Inklings is evidenced in C.S. Lewis' remarks concerning Williams, who he had known for only a short period of time. They became fast friends when Williams wrote Lewis a letter praising his book, The Allegory of Love. At the same time, Lewis had read Williams' book, The Place of the Lion and had sent him a like note commending his work, and they soon met afterwards. Of Williams, Lewis said, "Our friendship rapidly grew to the bone." When the Oxford University Press moved its offices from London to Oxford at the outset of the Second World War, their friendship grew all the more and Williams became a permanent member of the Inklings.

Williams remained, through his life, a faithful member of the Church of England. This is evident in his novels, War in Heaven, Descent into Hell and All Hallows' Eve. Williams passed away at the age of 58 on May 15, 1945, in Oxford. Even though he was mostly known for his novels, his headstone in Holywell Cemetery carries the single word: "poet.

Chapter 4
DAILY READINGS FOR ADVENT

DAY ONE

"I am the man, who with the utmost daring, discovered what has been discovered before."
G.K. Chesterton

The story of the coming and birth of the Christ Child is more than 2,000 years old. It has been told innumerable times by ministers, monks, teachers, doctors, waiters, cooks, gardeners, kings, tent makers, and countless voices of faith. It has transcended time, nationality, social status, denomination, and other things that tend to so easily separate us.

There is nothing new in the retelling of the story of Jesus' birth. From time to time someone may contrive a somewhat new slant on what they hope others would perceive as a new idea on the miracle of the ages. This is one story that has stood the test of time. It sets the standard for truth and the hope of our faith in God's promise to deliver us from our sins and from ourselves.

As Chesterton said, he had boldly found what had been found by so many before him. The only thing new about his discovery; was it was new to him, but even so, he had the courage to discover what had been reveled to so many, and now to him. That is one of the wonderful things about Advent; it becomes new to each one of us every year along with the renewal of God's promise to reconcile with us through his Son.

This Christmas, let us all discover what millions throughout the ages have discovered once again, the faith that began in a cold, damp stable and the child who changed the heart of the world.

DAILY READINGS:

Morning: Psalm 5:1-3

Give ear to my words, O Lord, consider my sighing. Listen to my cry for help, my King and my God, for to you I pray. In the morning, O Lord, you hear my voice; in the morning I lay my requests before you and wait in expectation.

Evening: 2 Corinthians 5:17

Therefore, if anyone is in Christ, he is a new creation; the old has gone, the new has come!

DAY TWO

"Continue seeking him with seriousness. Unless He wanted you, you would not be wanting Him."
C.S. Lewis

Last Christmas I saw an older gentleman wearing a bright red sweatshirt with a silhouette of the three wise men following the star of Bethlehem, above the picture were the words "Wise Men Still Seek Him." In seeing this, I wondered if this man was seeking Him, had found Him, or was just wearing a present he received last year. Whatever the case, the message was clear, that wise men and women still look for God's Son.

The tradition of the three wise men resonates throughout history. From the Christmas Carol "We Three Kings of Orient Are" to the hollow plastic figures on your neighbor's lawn, the story of the wise men has a central place in the heart of the Nativity Story. Even though the scriptures don't tell the exact number of the Magi, or if they were actually there on the night of Jesus' birth, tradition and truth tell the compelling story of the Kings from the East (Persia, now Iran), Balthazar, Melchior, and Caspar, who traveled the nearly 1,000-mile journey of faith.

But as Lewis stated, none of us seek God without Him first seeking us. The Magi followed the star because something (or someone) had actually been following them and in that leading them as well.

As they sought the miracle at the end of their journey, God was seeking the miracle of their hearts. The child they sought had been the impetus as well as the conclusion of their crossing.

So as we begin to seek Him this Christmas Season, let us all keep in mind that we would not be searching for Him if He had not sent us on the journey by searching and calling out for us first.

DAILY READINGS:

Morning: Psalm 34: 4-9

I sought the Lord, and he answered me; he delivered me from all my fears. Those who look to him are radiant; their faces are never covered with shame. This poor man called, and the Lord heard him; he saved him out of all his troubles. The angel of the Lord encamps around those who fear him, and he delivers them. Taste and see that the Lord is good; blessed are those who take refuge in him. Fear the Lord, you his holy people, for those who fear him lack nothing.

Evening: Matthew 2:1-2

After Jesus was born in Bethlehem in Judea, during the time of King Herod, Magi from the east came to Jerusalem and asked, "Where is the one who has been born king of the Jews? We saw his star when it rose and have come to worship him."

DAY THREE

"I admit you can practice Christianity without knowing much theology, just as you can drive a car without knowing much about internal combustion.

But when something breaks down in the car, you go humbly to the man who understands the works; whereas if something goes wrong with religion, you merely throw the works away and tell the theologian he is a liar."

Dorothy L. Sayers

It is possible that we take the burden of faith too much upon ourselves and look for guidance from those here on earth. We shape and adhere to our own philosophies and beliefs whether they actually hold true to God's Word or not. We tend to spend a lot of time making God in our own image rather than accepting the converse as true.

So when things start veering off course in our faith, we don't look to where we may have gone astray. Instead we look to the fallacy of the beliefs we created ourselves. We decide that we certainly can't be wrong, so it must be that God's Word is flawed somewhere. Since things aren't going as we had planned (that we are sure that our Creator had planned for us), it is easier for us to toss out the entire theology and find one that is more acceptable to the way we think things ought to be.

It is the utmost irony that so many times when something we own isn't working as it should, the first thing we hope is that maybe we are doing something wrong or don't have something set just right. Hopefully someone will be able to make a minor adjustment and put us back on course.

But in matters with eternal implications, we certainly can't be the ones who are off course, so we look for a theology or philosophy that fits our situation and makes us comfortable. It may hurt too much for God to set us straight.

As we look to the celebration of the birth of Christ, we should reconsider our own faith, and who and where we look to for it. This is the season not only of Advent, but the season to renew and simplify our faith and lay it at the foot of the manger. It is in this, that the infant dressed in rags that kings paid homage to so many ages ago can restore our faith.

DAILY READINGS:

Morning: II Chronicles 20: 20

Early in the morning they left for the Desert of Tekoa. As they set out, Jehoshaphat stood and said, "Listen to me, Judah and people of Jerusalem! Have faith in the lord your God and you will be upheld."

Evening: 1 Corinthians 2:1-5

And so it was with me, brothers and sisters. When I came to you, I did not come with eloquence or human wisdom as I proclaimed to you the testimony about God. For I resolved to know nothing while I was with you except Jesus Christ and him crucified. I came to you in weakness with great fear and trembling. My message and my preaching were not with wise and persuasive words, but with a demonstration of the Spirit's power, so that your faith might not rest on human wisdom, but on God's power.

DAY FOUR

"The Christ-child stood on Mary's knee,
His hair was like a crown,
and all the flowers looked up at Him,
and all the stars looked down."

> G.K. Chesterton

Thirty-three years after His birth in Bethlehem, as Saint Luke tells us in his Gospel, Jesus borrowed a donkey and rode into Jerusalem on what we now know as Palm Sunday. His triumphant entry into the Holy City was far removed from the circumstances of His birth. As the crowd cried "Hosanna" and the priests tried to silence them, Jesus quickly told them "I tell you," He replied, "If they keep quiet, the stones will cry out."

I am sure that the learned men of the Torah were somewhat startled at this itinerant preacher from the backwoods of Galilee who was stating that all of nature worships God and if men lost their voices, the very rocks beneath his feet would call out.

G.K. Chesterton never referred to nature as "Mother Nature" but as "Brother Nature" believing that we both have the same Father. So then, it is not difficult to believe that if Christ himself laid witness to nature's praise, that Chesterton captured the wonder of nature's worship at the beginning of Jesus' earthly life.

Whether we are as the flowers looking up, or the stars looking down, our nature is that of all creation, to bow in awe of this child that was born In Bethlehem.

DAILY READINGS:

Morning: Psalms 148:1-6

Praise the Lord from the heavens; praise him in the heights above. Praise him, all his angels; praise him, all his heavenly hosts. Praise him, sun and moon; praise him, all you shining stars. Praise him, you highest heavens and you waters above the skies. Let them praise the name of the Lord, for at his command they were created, and he established them forever and ever.

Evening: Luke 12: 27

Consider how the wild flowers grow. They do not labor or spin. Yet, I tell you, not even Solomon in all his splendor was dressed like one of these.

DAY FIVE

"You can only come to the morning through the shadows."

J.R.R. Tolkien

The scriptures talk a lot about light. From God's first words in Genesis, "Let there be light," to Jesus telling us in the Gospels that He is the light of the world. In Isaiah 9:2 the prophet says, "The people walking in darkness have seen a great light; on those living in the land of the shadow of death a light has dawned." Light gives us hope.

Isaiah and Tolkien have come to the same conclusion. If we are seeking the light, we probably have been spending our time in darkness whether we know it or not. Just because our eyes may be used to the shadows and we don't trip and fall as much as we had before, doesn't mean that we had been walking in the light. Tolkien's morning light or Isaiah's great light is only seen by walking out of the shadows.

Our shadows may not necessarily be actually physical darkness, but it is as real just the same. The shadows in our heart that invade our souls keep us groping and stumbling toward whatever light we can catch a glimpse of - no matter if it is actually the light or just a reflection of something else. The great light we all yearn for can be found in only one place.

The Bethlehem Star still beckons as its light pales next to the one whose birth it proclaims. The light is all around us, we just have to look with the right set of eyes.

DAILY READINGS:

Morning: Isaiah 9:1-2

Nevertheless, there will be no more gloom for those who were in distress. In the past he humbled the land of Zebulon and the land of Naphtali, but in the future he will honor Galilee of the nations, by the Way of the Sea, beyond the Jordan. The people walking in darkness have seen a great light; on those living in the land of deep darkness, a light has dawned.

Evening: Romans 13: 11-12

And do this, understanding the present time. The hour has already come for you to wake up from your slumber, because our salvation is nearer now than when we first believed. The night is nearly over; the day is almost here. So let us put aside the deeds of darkness and put on the armor of light.

DAY SIX

"Miracles are a retelling in small letters of the very same story which is written across the whole world in letters too large for some of us to see."

C.S. Lewis

There is no miracle more astonishing than the incarnation. Think about the creator of the universe whose name is unpronounceable, the beginning and the end, the Great I Am, becoming one of his own creations in the form of a baby born to a poor young couple. It was He, who spoke the world into existence, created the stars, the oceans, and the molecules that give substance to everything.

These are all miracles of the grandest scale. For centuries man has stood solemn at creation, pondering these vast miracles. No matter how magnificent, the letters may have been too large for us to see. But God had another plan and as Lewis thought, retold the story of creation, glory, and redemption in letters of lower case; small enough for us to see and hold as an infant in a manger and large enough to deliver us from our sins.

DAILY READINGS:

Morning: Isaiah 7:13-14

Then Isaiah said, "Hear now, you house of David! Is it not enough to try the patience of human beings? Will you try the patience of my God also? Therefore the Lord himself will give you a sign: The virgin will conceive and give birth to a son, and will call him Emmanuel."

Evening: Luke 2:1-7

In those days Caesar Augustus issued a decree that a census should be taken of the entire Roman world. (This was the first census that took place while Quirinius was governor of Syria.) And everyone went to their own town to register. So Joseph also went up from the town of Nazareth in Galilee to Judea, to Bethlehem the town of David, because he belonged to the house and line of David. He went there to register with Mary, who was pledged to be married to him and was expecting a child. While they were there, the time came for the baby to be born, and she gave birth to her firstborn, a son. She wrapped him in cloths and placed him in a manger, because there was no guest room available for them.

DAY SEVEN

"I was thinking just last Sunday that the world confuses one day with the rest throughout the year, and that one day is the day that a child appeared."
Larry Norman

The older we get the faster time seems to go. One day quickly turns into the next and weeks turn into months and then into years. As the calendar swirls around our heads, it is easy to confuse one day with another. How many times have we had to stop and think, "what day is it?" Is today Tuesday? No wait that was yesterday. So many times so many days just seem the same.

But there is one day that is not like the rest. The day we celebrate the birth of Jesus is not like any other day. The day that the child appeared altered human history and turned the universe inside out. The Creator made Himself known in the most humble and powerful way.

As Dr. William Cummings wrote in Hark the Herald Angels Sing, God and sinners have been reconciled; reconciled on the day that this child appeared. If the world confuses this one-day with the rest throughout the year, we certainly can't, not in light of the story that began in Bethlehem.

DAILY READINGS:

Morning: Jeremiah 31: 34

No longer will they teach their neighbors, or say to one another, 'Know the Lord,' because they will all know me, from the least of them to the greatest," declares the Lord. "For I will forgive their wickedness and will remember their sins no more.

Evening: Luke 1: 68-79

Praise be to the Lord, the God of Israel, because he has come to his people and redeemed them. He has raised up a horn of salvation for us in the house of his servant David (as he said through his holy prophets of long ago), salvation from our enemies and from the hand of all who hate us — to show mercy to our ancestors and to remember his holy covenant, the oath he swore to our father Abraham: to rescue us from the hand of our enemies, and to enable us to serve him without fear in holiness and righteousness before him all our day. And you, my child, will be called a prophet of the Most High; for you will go on before the Lord to prepare the way for him, to give his people the knowledge of salvation through the forgiveness of their sins because of the tender mercy of our God, by which the rising sun will come to us from heaven to shine on those living in darkness and in the shadow of death, to guide our feet into the path of peace.

DAY EIGHT

"When we set out I did not believe that Jesus is the Son of God, and when we reached the zoo I did."
                                                                C.S. Lewis

C.S. Lewis' trip to the Whipsnade Zoo one Sunday morning in September of 1929 culminated a nearly life-long search for the truth. Riding in the sidecar of his brother Warnie's motorcycle, this 30-mile ride from Oxford not only changed his life, but the millions who would come to read his works, who, like him, questioned God's existence and Jesus' deity.

The trip to the zoo came a few days after a long discussion with J.R.R. Tolkien. It was during this conversation that he overcame the last remnants of doubts and subsequent arguments against Christianity. In just a few short moments, riding through the English countryside, he went from unbelief to belief.

This was a far cry from a Damascus Road conversion; it was just a quiet change of heart to end a long intellectual search, in the sidecar of an old motorcycle on the way to the zoo. Lewis' conversion has always struck me as one of the most profound stories of the realization of belief in the annals of Christianity.

I am always surprised at how God touches those who seek Him; some by an emotional upheaval, some by the call of a quiet voice, and some by a logical realization.

But it is the same God that calls us individually where we are and presents us with a choice of eternal consequences. Mary, Joseph, the shepherds, the Magi, and even King Herod were presented with the choice given by God through the infant in a manger. This Christmas the choice is before us anew.

Like Lewis, with God's grace, we can all say, "When I started out I didn't believe that Jesus is the Son of God, and when I got to the manger I did."

DAILY READINGS:

Morning: I Kings 19:11-13

Then a great and powerful wind tore the mountains apart and shattered the rocks before the Lord, but the Lord was not in the wind. After the wind there was an earthquake, but the Lord was not in the earthquake. After the earthquake came a fire, but the Lord was not in the fire. And after the fire came a gentle whisper. When Elijah heard it, he pulled his cloak over his face and went out and stood at the mouth of the cave.

Evening: Acts 2:21-22

And everyone who calls on the name of the Lord will be saved. People of Israel, listen to this: Jesus of Nazareth was a man accredited by God to you by miracles, wonders and signs, which God did among you through him, as you yourselves know.

DAY NINE

"The principle part of faith is patience."

George MacDonald

I don't think I have met anyone who really likes to wait. Some people don't mind it so much, but I don't believe that I know anyone who, when having their druthers, would choose waiting over having their wishes filled right now. With a culture of internet, sound bites, 24-hour news, e-mail, and fast food, we are used to not waiting and find ourselves getting frustrated or even angry when we do find ourselves having to wait. If our computer takes too long to boot up or if we have to wait more than a few minutes in line at McDonald's, we feel our patience waning and our nerves start to get on edge.

One of my grandmother's favorite sayings was "patience is a virtue." When I would ask her what a virtue was, she took her time and explained that a virtue was a good or desirable quality and that patience would keep my soul. I find myself more patient as I grow older, but only on my better days.

In reading the great author George MacDonald's words, I can't help but think of the unbelievable patience that those who waited the long years between the fall of Adam and Eve and the first Christmas. Countless thousands had waited their entire lives in hope of their Savior arriving during their time on earth to deliver them from their burdens and the oppression in which they were living.

But finally, after thousands of years, this one child was born in the smallest of villages; in a stable among cows and sheep. The wait was finally over and God's promise fulfilled. Fulfilled in His time as their faith was rewarded, the redeemer had come.

So as we wait in line somewhere this Christmas season, let's not forget amidst all the waiting, we are most fortunate that the waiting for our redeemer is over and He is as close as our hearts.

DAILY READINGS:

Morning: Psalms 130:1-6

Out of the depths I cry to you, Lord, Lord, hear my voice. Let your ears be attentive to my cry for mercy. If you, Lord, kept a record of sins, Lord, who could stand? But with you there is forgiveness, so that we can, with reverence, serve you. I wait for the Lord, my whole being waits, and in his word I put my hope.

Evening: Titus 2:11-14

For the grace of God has appeared that offers salvation to all people. It teaches us to say "No" to ungodliness and worldly passions, and to live self-controlled, upright and godly lives in this present age, while we wait for the blessed hope - the appearing of the glory of our great God and Savior, Jesus Christ, who gave himself for us to redeem us from all wickedness and to purify for himself a people that are his very own, eager to do what is good.

DAY TEN

"The simplification of anything is always sensational."

G.K. Chesterton

Through the centuries of those awaiting the coming of the Savior, most, if not all, were waiting for a king that actually looked like a king; a king with flowing robes, majestic horses, and attendants who were righteous and who would set them free.

God could have chosen this path, but the story would not have been the same; in fact, it would be much like many other stories of deliverance when a good and noble king rescues his people. An epic tale, but not necessarily what one would call sensational - a tale of emancipation, but not necessarily one of deliverance.

But for the king, who in thirty-three short years would deliver mankind, to arrive as a baby had turned the everyday act of the birth of a child into the most sensational event in history.

DAILY READINGS:

Morning: Isaiah 9:6-7

For to us a child is born, to us a son is given, and the government will be on his shoulders. And he will be called Wonderful Counselor, Mighty God, Everlasting Father, and Prince of Peace. Of the increase of his government and peace there will be no end. He will reign on David's throne and over his kingdom, establishing and upholding it with justice and righteousness from that time on and forever. The zeal of the Lord Almighty will accomplish this.

Evening: Matthew 1:18-25

This is how the birth of Jesus the Messiah came about: His mother Mary was pledged to be married to Joseph, but before they came together, she was found to be pregnant through the Holy Spirit. Because Joseph her husband was a righteous man and did not want to expose her to public disgrace, he had mind to divorce her quietly. But after he had considered this, an angel of the Lord appeared to him in a dream and said, "Joseph, son of David, do not be afraid to take Mary home as your wife, because what is conceived in her is from the Holy Spirit. She will give birth to a son, and you are to give him the name Jesus, because he will save his people from their sins." All this took place to fulfill what the Lord had said through the prophet: "The virgin will conceive and give birth to a son, and they will call him Emmanuel" (which means "God with us").

DAY ELEVEN

"God hides nothing. His very work from the beginning is revelation - a casting aside of veil after veil, a showing unto men of truth after truth. On and on from fact Divine He advances, until at length in His Son Jesus He unveils His very face."

George MacDonald

Growing up, I had often heard so many talk of how mysterious God was. His mind, His will, and His thoughts were so far above what we could comprehend. The best we could do was to hope we were on the right track, do the right thing, and hope for the best in some kind of celestial and spiritual roulette. And if we were lucky, we would make it through.

But here George McDonald, the 19th-century pastor, novelist, teacher, and fantasy writer, had an insight to God that opened the hearts of millions, including C.S. Lewis, and that helped light the path of faith in Christ. The paradox of the mystery of God lies in the fact that He reveals Himself in everything around us.

The stars, the flowers, the dust on the road all speak to God's presence. Truth is all around us because God is all around us, but we so often miss it because we are looking in the wrong direction or we don't know what we are looking for at all. We look for God where we think He is or where we expect Him to be.

He shouts to us, "I Am," and we respond, "Yeah, but I am going to look over here where the light is more to my liking." And while the world is searching for where we hope God will be, He has already revealed His face to the ages in the face of the child born in Bethlehem who would redeem us all.

DAILY READINGS:

Morning: Amos 4:13

He who forms the mountains, who creates the wind, and who reveals his thoughts to mortals, who turns dawn to darkness, and treads on the heights of the earth.

Evening: II Corinthians 2: 9-13

However, as it is written: "What no eye has seen, what no ear has heard, and what no human mind has conceived - these things God has prepared for those who love him" for God has revealed them to us by his Spirit. The Spirit searches all things, even the deep things of God. For who knows a person's thoughts except that person's own spirit within? In the same way no one knows the thoughts of God except the Spirit of God. We have not received the spirit of the world but the Spirit who is from God, that we may understand what God has freely given us. This is what we speak, not in words taught us by human wisdom but in words taught by the Spirit, explaining spiritual realities with Spirit-taught words.

DAY TWELVE

"For here is spiritual pride, the ultimate sin, in action - the sin of believing in one's own righteousness. The true prophet says humbly, "To me, a sinful man, God spoke." But the scribes and Pharisees declare, "When we speak, God agrees." They feel no need of a special revelation, for they are always, in their own view, infallible. It is this self-righteousness of the pious that most breeds atheism, by inspiring all decent, ordinary men with loathing of the enormous lie."

Joy Davidman

C.S. Lewis wrote that all sin comes from pride. Here his wife reminds us that pride clouds our judgment. Pride dilutes our reason. Pride hardens our hearts. It is dangerous in the secular world and devastating in the spiritual world.

Pride does not just keep us from growing in our faith; it destroys it in a most horrific way. Pride leads us to believe that God's words and ours are the same. It moves us from saying, "God's standards are my standards" to "My standards are God's standards." Pride misleads us in believing that we are not merely God's creation but we somehow are now on the same level.

In the Nativity story, pride is played out as well. Caesar thought himself as God. The possibility of a Savior, the Son of God, being born on his watch was unthinkable and Judea wasn't big enough for both of them. In seeing himself as divine, he missed the one who was.

We run the risk of doing the same as Caesar did. Being close to God and believing we are next to God is not the same thing. In fact, they are polar opposites. Thinking we are next to God, that is being on the same level of spirituality, does nothing but keep us away from the one with whom we long to be close.

We all must take care in this Christmas season, as we come to adore the Christ Child and renew our faith. We need to let God be God and follow Him where he leads us. Pride rarely comes as an onslaught, but as a stealthily growing spiritual malignancy. If we think it can't happen to us; it already has.

DAILY READINGS:

Morning: Daniel 10:10-12

A hand touched me and set me trembling on my hands and knees. He said, "Daniel, you who are highly esteemed, consider carefully the words I am about to speak to you, and stand up, for I have now been sent to you." And when he said this to me, I stood up trembling. Then he continued, "Do not be afraid, Daniel. Since the first day that you set your mind to gain understanding and to humble yourself before your God, your words were heard, and I have come in response to them.

Evening: Romans 12:1-3

Therefore, I urge you, brothers and sisters, in view of God's mercy, to offer your bodies as a living sacrifice, holy and pleasing to God — this is true worship. Do not conform to the pattern of this world, but be transformed by the renewing of your mind. Then you will be able to test and approve what God's will is — his good, pleasing and perfect will. For by the grace given me I say to every one of you: Do not think of yourself more highly than you ought, but rather think of yourself with sober judgment, in accordance with the faith God has distributed to each of you.

DAY THIRTEEN

"It is not possible to be 'incidentally a Christian.'
The fact of Christianity must be overwhelmingly first or nothing."

Sheldon Vanauken

Vanauken doesn't give much leeway here. But he writes an indelible truth; it is not possible to be an "Oh by the way, I am a Christian" Christian. When one comes to believe in Jesus, he or she becomes a new person, not so much a changed person, but a new one just as new as the day they were born.

No one can be incidentally a man or a woman. It is who we are. It is the same as when we become a believer in Christ. It becomes who we are, not just what we are, as in nationality, a member of an organization or club, or denomination.

He also reminds us that our Christianity has to be overwhelmingly first. Not just first above all else, but devastatingly first. Over powering first, the primary reason for all we do, think, and are. Not just first where there are second things, third things and beyond. Crushingly first where there is no visible second or third things. In doing this all things that follow are brighter, kinder, and have more meaning.

Christianity being intensely first means that everything else can be touched by the love that Jesus has given us. Him being first only gives us the overflowing love that He first gave to the earth in a gift that none of us deserve but that we all so desperately need; His Son that gave life to all who believe. If Jesus is not first, he is not second, third, fourth, fiftieth, or even last. He is nothing at all.

DAILY READINGS:

Morning: Job 23:11-12

My feet have closely followed his steps. I have kept to his way without turning aside. I have not departed from the commands of his lips; I have treasured the words of his mouth more than my daily bread.

Evening: I Corinthians 15:58

Therefore, my dear brothers and sisters, stand firm. Let nothing move you. Always give yourselves fully to the work of the Lord, because you know that your labor in the Lord is not in vain.

DAY FOURTEEN

"God has landed on this enemy-occupied world in human form...the perfect surrender and humiliation was undergone by Christ perfect because He was God, surrender and humiliation because He was man."

C.S. Lewis

The definition of irony is that the actual result of what happens is the total opposite of the expected. While those who awaited a Savior were looking for their king to arrive and obliterate their enemies and destroy the chains that kept them in slavery, God imposed the ultimate irony on mankind. No king on a thundering steed, but a defenseless baby born to a young couple from a town that the rest of Judea laughed about or discarded completely. "Can anything good come from Nazareth?"

But the irony goes much further than that. It is almost impossible to imagine that the creator would want to transform Himself to be part of His creation. The Supreme Being yielding his power to become powerless and putting His plan of love and forgiveness in the hands of Joseph and Mary in the heart of enemy territory.

If any of us do not think that this world was a hostile place to the newborn Son of God, all we have to do is recall the death of the Holy Innocents when King Herod ordered all children two years old and younger killed when he heard of Jesus' birth.

God did not surrender to us, but to redeem us and bring us back to Him. The humiliation He endured was the holy becoming flesh, born in a stable, and lay in a feeding trough. In this Christmastide, we all should remember not just the miracle of God becoming man, but the utmost act of surrender that he did for all men and look to what we have to surrender to Him to continue the story.

DAILY READINGS:

Morning: Psalm 37:3-7

Trust in the Lord and do good; dwell in the land and enjoy safe pasture. Take delight in the Lord and he will give you the desires of your heart. Commit your way to the Lord; trust in him and he will do this: He will make your righteous reward shine like the dawn, your vindication like the noonday sun. Be still before the Lord and wait patiently for him.

Evening: James 1:2-4

Consider it pure joy, my brothers and sisters, whenever you face trials of many kinds, because you know that the testing of your faith produces perseverance. Let perseverance finish its work so that you may be mature and complete, not lacking anything.

DAY FIFTEEN

"I'm a Christian, and every song I've written is a Christian song."

Larry Norman

Larry Norman saw the world through spiritual eyes. To him there was no way to divide his life into Christian and secular parts. His faith defined him and all that he did, said, and wrote. His songs chronicled the human experience, running the gamut from love, loss, and faith to humor, life's questions, and God's presence. But no matter what he wrote and sang about, it was always about God. He may have been singing about burying his sister in sand on the beach, being a servant, eating at a diner in Texas, or the Messiah's return - it was all the same to him... it was all about Jesus.

G.K. Chesterton had once remarked that it didn't matter if you were talking about pigs or the stars, you were still talking about God. If God is indeed in our hearts all we do is related to our faith and life in him. Whether we are in church, in the grocery store, or having dinner at Outback, it is all because of Him. We should take great care in how we act and react in all we do.

We do not have on and off days in being Christians. It is not dictated by if "we feel like it" on a particular day. If we are Christians that is who we are; all the time and all we do is viewed through the prism of the cross and the manger, by us and all those around us.

The world was never the same after the Nativity and neither are we. We need to pray for that revelation this Advent, and that each day we can see God in everything we see and those that see us will see Him too.

DAILY READINGS:

Morning: II Chronicles 31:20-21

This is what Hezekiah did throughout Judah, doing what was good and right and faithful before the Lord his God. In everything that he undertook in the service of God's temple and in obedience to the law and the commands, he sought his God and worked wholeheartedly. And so he prospered.

Evening: Galatians 2:20-21

I have been crucified with Christ and I no longer live, but Christ lives in me. The life I now live in the body, I live by faith in the Son of God, who loved me and gave himself for me. I do not set aside the grace of God.

DAY SIXTEEN

"All we have to decide is what to do with the time that is given to us."

J.R.R. Tolkien

I don't know if anyone actually knows when mankind became interested in measuring time. Early man kept the largest calendar of all, using God's creation of the sun, moon, stars and planets to measure the time as it passed. Early civilizations relied on the motion of these celestial bodies to help determine days, months, and the seasons of the year.

But as life became more complicated, we thought we needed to dissect time into smaller pieces. A year, month, or even a day was not diminutive enough for us to divide our time on earth. We needed hours, minutes, and seconds.

Historians believe that the earliest sun-dials were developed around 3500 BC in Egypt to break our day down to "manageable' increments and soon found their way above the doorways in most homes, and by the 10th century various pocket sun dials were used throughout civilization. By the 1500s spring driven clocks were invented in Germany and our obsession with time was off and running.

Now we have atomic clocks, hundred thousand dollar wristwatches, PDAs, electronic reminders, and clocks on our cell phones. Everything we need to keep track of our years and minutes here on earth. We have everything that money can buy to help us keep track of time, except what it can't.

The difficult part is not knowing what time it is; the difficult part is deciding what we are to do with the time that we have presented to us. We certainly don't know the number of years, months, days, minutes or seconds God has allotted us on earth.

Many are destined to die young, while others live to what is considered to be an old age.

Time belongs to God, not to us, but what does belong to us is the decision of what we are to do with the gift of time we have been given. The scriptures say that God has numbered our days and we have much good to do, if we choose before they end.

In the center of all the ages is the birth of the Christ Child where eternity touched us all and gave time a new dimension and the possibility that God will make our time His, if we seek Him and open our hearts.

DAILY READINGS:

Morning: Psalm 25:1-7

In you, Lord my God, I put my trust. I trust in you; do not let me be put to shame, nor let my enemies triumph over me. No one who hopes in you will ever be put to shame, but shame will come on those who are treacherous without cause. Show me your ways, Lord, teach me your paths. Guide me in your truth and teach me, for you are God my Savior, and my hope is in you all day long. Remember, Lord, your great mercy and love, for they are from of old. Do not remember the sins of my youth and my rebellious ways; according to your love remember me, for you, Lord, are good.

Evening: Matthew 25:14-28

Again, it will be like a man going on a journey, who called his servants and entrusted his wealth to them. To one he gave five bags of gold, to another two bags, and to another one bag, each according to his ability. Then he went on his journey. The man who had received five bags of gold went at once and put his money to work and gained five bags more. So also, the one with two bags of gold gained two more. But the man who had received one bag went off, dug a hole in the ground and hid his master's money. After a long time the master of those servants returned and settled accounts with them. The man who had received five bags of gold brought the other five. "Master," he said, "you entrusted me with five bags of gold. See, I have gained five more."

His master replied, "Well done, good and faithful servant! You have been faithful with a few things; I will put you in charge of many things. Come and share your master's happiness!" The man with two bags of gold also came. "Master," he said, "you entrusted me with two bags of gold; see, I have gained two more." His master replied, "Well done, good and faithful servant! You have been faithful with a few things; I will put you in charge of many things. Come and share your master's happiness!"

Then the man who had received one bag of gold came. "Master," he said, "I knew that you are a hard man, harvesting where you have not sown and gathering where you have not scattered seed. So I was afraid and went out and hid your gold in the ground. See, here is what belongs to you." His master replied, "You wicked, lazy servant! So you knew that I harvest where I have not sown and gather where I have not scattered seed? Well then, you should have put my money on deposit with the bankers, so that when I returned, I would have received it back with interest. Take the bag of gold from him and give it to the one who has ten bags. For those who have will be given more, and they will have abundance. As for those who do not have, even what they have will be taken from them. And throw that worthless servant outside, into the darkness, where there will be weeping and gnashing of teeth."

DAY SEVENTEEN

"Anyone thinking of the Holy Child as born in December would mean by it exactly what we mean by it; that Christ is not merely a summer sun of the prosperous but a winter fire for the unfortunate."

G.K. Chesterton

It is always surprising at how various Christians view God; some as a stern taskmaster and judge, some as a loving father, and some as a personal friend. It isn't hard to see that there is some truth in each of these images. But I have met a number of Christians (some of whom have been close friends) that see the Creator of the Universe as some sort of holy errand boy that is only there to satisfy all of our material wants as to show how much He loves us and how much we are in His favor. We see Him as a mystical servant that not only created us and died to save us, but only wants us to be happy and will provide for our every whim.

There certainly is no sin in being prosperous, although I don't think because anyone is well off financially they have curried God's favor more than someone who is not. They have a great responsibility to use the means God has bestowed on them for the benefit of others. I am most fortunate to know a few individuals and families whose heart for God has only fostered their concern and compassion for others. They use their wealth to reach those in need.

Some years ago, I saw a mega-church's television ad for their upcoming "Broadway Christmas Spectacular" which they seemed proud to let everyone know the "Broadway Style Budget" they incurred in bringing the message of the birth of Christ to our small community.

They did open the doors one evening for the homeless, elderly, and others who were less fortunate for the dress rehearsal before the show was opened for the rest of us. I know that this is done in countless congregations and this in itself is not the problem.

But it does run the risk of directing thoughts to the Christ of the summer sun of the prosperous, helping us think "look at the wonderful thing we have done for Jesus this Christmas in entertaining so many with the story of His birth. The bigger the better and we must have His Blessing as it was so successful."

I believe that we are not blessed because of something we have done, we are blessed so we can do greater things. God doesn't give His blessings as rewards, He gives His blessings as resources to reach out and to help and serve others.

With all this tinsel and red and green lights, it is easy to lose the Child whose birth we celebrate in December as the true winter fire that comforts and warms the unfortunate and those who cry out to the Son of God to forgive their sins, mend their hearts, and heal their souls.

This Christmas as we view so many plays and celebrations presented to us, let us pray that the Child of the winter fire out-shines the one of the summer sun and that we realize that we are all the same in the eyes and hands of the Christ Child.

DAILY READINGS:

Morning: Psalm 61:1-8

Hear my cry, O God; listen to my prayer. From the ends of the earth I call to you, I call as my heart grows faint; lead me to the rock that is higher than I. For you have been my refuge, a strong tower against the foe. I long to dwell in your tent forever and take refuge in the shelter of your wings. For you, God, have heard my vows; you have given me the heritage of those who fear your name. Increase the days of the king's life, his years for many generations. May he be enthroned in God's presence forever; appoint your love and faithfulness to protect him. Then I will ever sing in praise of your name and fulfill my vows day after day.

Evening: Matthew 11:25-28

At that time Jesus said, "I praise you, Father, Lord of heaven and earth, because you have hidden these things from the wise and learned, and revealed them to little children. Yes, Father, for this was your good pleasure.

All things have been committed to me by my Father. No one knows the Son except the Father, and no one knows the Father except the Son and those to whom the Son chooses to reveal him. Come to me, all you who are weary and burdened, and I will give you rest. Take my yoke upon you and learn from me, for I am gentle and humble in heart, and you will find rest for your souls. For my yoke is easy and my burden is light."

DAY EIGHTEEN

"I think in order to move forward into the future, you need to know where you've been."

Charles Williams

One of the magical and wonderfully mystical things about Advent is that it allows all who wish, the opportunity to do two things. It is a perfect time to reflect on the joyous memories of Christmases past with family and friends that have gone before us and those who are with us still, and it gives us the occasion to look forward to the coming year and the calling and opportunities that God is setting before us. The past and the future intersect as we anticipate the coming of the Christ Child on Christmas.

No matter who we are or who we are becoming, it is impossible to know ourselves fully without having some knowledge of the journey that has brought us to where we are. The scriptures tell us that, "In his heart a man charts his course, but the Lord directs his steps." And if each of our steps is directed by God, how much more important is it that we look at where we have been, where He has lead us to find the faith and strength to grasp the future that God has for us?

Knowing that God has been with us in the past should help give us the faith and peace to trust Him and move toward the future. But in order to do that we must not only look back to where we have been, but to where God has been for all of us to have a future, a future that began in Bethlehem.

DAILY READINGS:

Morning: Proverbs 3:1-8

My son, do not forget my teaching, but keep my commands in your heart, for they will prolong your life many years and bring you peace and prosperity. Let love and faithfulness never leave you; bind them around your neck, write them on the tablet of your heart. Then you will win favor and a good name in the sight of God and humankind. Trust in the Lord with all your heart and lean not on your own understanding; in all your ways submit to him, and he will make your paths straight. Do not be wise in your own eyes; fear the Lord and shun evil. This will bring health to your body and nourishment to your bones.

Evening: John 16:12-15

"I have much more to say to you, more than you can now bear. But when he, the Spirit of truth, comes, he will guide you into all the truth. He will not speak on his own; he will speak only what he hears, and he will tell you what is yet to come. He will glorify me because it is from me that he will receive what he will make known to you. All that belongs to the Father is mine. That is why I said the Spirit will receive from me what he will make known to you."

DAY NINETEEN

"Official Christianity, of late years, has been having what is known as bad press. We are constantly assured that the churches are empty because preachers insist too much upon doctrine — dull dogma as people call it. The fact is quite the opposite. It is the neglect of dogma that makes for dullness. The Christian faith is the most exciting drama that ever staggered the imagination of man and the dogma is the drama."

Dorothy Sayers

The drama of the Gospel leaves nothing wanting to any of us who truly take the time to read it and think about what it is that we are reading. The word Gospel itself means "good news" and the good news begins with the story of a young woman who, in the presence of Gabriel - a being who stands in the presence of God Himself, was troubled by the angel telling her that she was highly favored and that the Lord was with her.

Here was a young woman, perhaps fifteen years old or so, having a conversation with one of the most awesome creations that God had made concerning the fate of mankind.

And that is where the dogma begins - the belief that a young virgin was singled out by the creator of the universe to deliver the child that would deliver all of us. The belief that Mary chose God's plan for her as she said "be it done to me according to your word" and set forth in motion the series of events that would redeem the human race.

The belief that Mary's son would one day heal the sick, walk on water, raise the dead, die and conquer death so we could as well is hardly a dull tale.

DAILY READINGS:

Morning: Isaiah 7:13-17

Then Isaiah said, "Hear now, you house of David! Is it not enough to try the patience of human beings? Will you try the patience of my God also? Therefore the Lord himself will give you a sign: The virgin will conceive and give birth to a son, and will call him Emmanuel. He will be eating curds and honey when he knows enough to reject the wrong and choose the right, for before the boy knows enough to reject the wrong and choose the right, the land of the two kings you dread will be laid waste. The Lord will bring on you and on your people and on the house of your father a time unlike any since Ephraim broke away from Judah—he will bring the king of Assyria.

Evening: Luke 1:26-38

In the sixth month of Elizabeth's pregnancy, God sent the angel Gabriel to Nazareth, a town in Galilee, to a virgin pledged to be married to a man named Joseph, a descendant of David. The virgin's name was Mary. The angel went to her and said, "Greetings, you who are highly favored! The Lord is with you." Mary was greatly troubled at his words and wondered what kind of greeting this might be. But the angel said to her, "Do not be afraid, Mary, you have found favor with God. You will conceive and give birth to a son, and you are to call him Jesus. He will be great and will be called the Son of the Most High. The Lord God will give him the throne of his father David, and he will reign over the house of Jacob forever; his kingdom will never end."

"How will this be," Mary asked the angel, "since I am a virgin?" The angel answered, "The Holy Spirit will come on you, and the power of the Most High will overshadow you. So the holy one to be born will be called the Son of God.

Even Elizabeth your relative is going to have a child in her old age, and she who was said to be unable to conceive is in her sixth month. For no word from God will ever fail." "I am the Lord's servant," Mary answered. "May it be to me according to your word." Then the angel left her.

DAY TWENTY

"If you read history you will find that the Christians who did most in the present world were precisely those who thought most of the next. It is since Christians have largely ceased to think of the other world that they have become so ineffective in this."

C.S. Lewis

God always seems to do things backwards from the way things are done in this world. Saying the last will be first, the meek will inherit the earth, and one must lose their life to save it, makes no earthly sense at all, but then again it isn't supposed to. As Christians we know that this world is not our final stop, we are here for a short time with another world waiting.

Here Lewis takes an important look at not just the early church, but the impact that the apostles, martyrs, theologians, and reformers had on history. They literally changed the world because they thought more of where they were going than where they were. Again, it is God doing things contrary to earthly principles and beliefs. I don't know if the world holds more distractions today than in the early days of Christianity or the fact that we allow ourselves to be more distracted.

But whatever the case, the less we think about the world to come, the less we actually care about the one we live in now. We may, indeed, think of the distractions this world offers and find the result that we are thinking less of Heaven and thus watering down our service to this world and those who God calls us to serve.

Advent gives us another chance to set our thoughts on the world to come, the one that the Christ Child ushered in that dark night in Bethlehem, and in doing so, do more for the one we live in now.

DAILY READINGS:

Morning: Psalms 10:10:14

Arise, Lord! Lift up your hand, O God. Do not forget the helpless. Why do the wicked revile God? Why do they say to them- selves "He won't call us to account?" But you, God, see the trouble of the afflicted; you consider their grief and take it in hand. The victims commit themselves to you; you are the helper of the fatherless .This is what Hezekiah did throughout Judah, doing what was good and right and faithful before the Lord his God. In everything that he undertook in the service of God's temple and in obedience to the law and the commands, he sought his God and worked wholeheartedly. And so he prospered.

Evening: I Peter 4:7-11

The end of all things is near. Therefore be alert and of sober mind so that you may pray. Above all, love each other deeply, because love covers over a multitude of sins. Offer hospitality to one another without grumbling. Each of you should use whatever gift you have received to serve others, as faithful stewards of God's grace in its various forms. If you speak, you should do so as one who speaks the very words of God. If you serve, you should do so with the strength God provides, so that in all things God may be praised through Jesus Christ. To him be the glory and the power for ever and ever. Amen.

DAY TWENTY-ONE

"With a love like yours,
A man could live in beauty and in grace,
If I were a king,
I'd give everything just to see your face,
With a love like yours a man cold be completely satisfied,
He'd have no more fears, he'd shed no more tears,
and have no more need to hide ..."
                                  Larry Norman

The Greek word Agape is defined as the unconditional, self-sacrificing, and divine love of God. This is vastly different from Philia that is brotherly love and Eros which denotes physical love. In experiencing and thinking of God's love (Agape), especially during the Christmas season, it is easy to take to heart the first line in this song written by Larry Norman.

It is in God's unreserved love and only in God's love that anyone can find true beauty, grace, and peace. Nothing else can fill the longing of our heart and the emptiness of our soul but God's absolute love. And there is no doubt that once it is realized, that we would, even if we were kings, give everything just to see the face of which divine love radiates. I am sure many righteous kings throughout the centuries would have gladly traded their kingdoms and all that was in them for that opportunity to see God's face. In the presence of God's love all else becomes meaningless.

With the embrace of God's love, there remains nothing left to seek. It is all encompassing and the light of His love drives out any fears and dries the tears of loneliness and sorrow, if only we will let it. There is, indeed, no more need to hide, as it is impossible to hide in the light.

DAILY READINGS:

Morning: Psalms 63:1-5

You, God, are my God, earnestly I seek you; I thirst for you, my whole being longs for you, in a dry and parched land where there is no water. I have seen you in the sanctuary and beheld your power and your glory. Because your love is better than life, my lips will glorify you. I will praise you as long as I live, and in your name I will lift up my hands. I will be fully satisfied as with the richest of foods.

Evening: Acts 17: 24-28

The God who made the world and everything in it is the Lord of heaven and earth and does not live in temples built by hands. And he is not served by human hands, as if he needed anything. Rather, he himself gives everyone life and breath and everything else. From one man he made all the nations, that they should inhabit the whole earth; and he marked out their appointed times in history and the boundaries of their lands. God did this so that they would seek him and perhaps reach out for him and find him, though he is not far from any one of us.

DAY TWENTY-TWO

"The best argument for Christianity is Christians: their joy, their certainty, their completeness. But the strongest argument against Christianity is also Christians – when they are somber and joyless, when they are self-righteous and smug in complacent consecration, when they are narrow and repressive, then Christianity dies a thousand deaths. But, though it is just to condemn some Christians for these things, perhaps, after all, it is not just, though very easy, to condemn Christianity itself for them. Indeed, there are impressive indications that the positive quality of joy is in Christianity and possibly nowhere else."

Sheldon Vanauken

There is an important thing that we get to choose when we become a Christian. We have to choose what type of Christian we will be. Will we be of the former type of which Vanauken speaks with joy and certainty or join the ranks of the latter who are self-righteous, joyless, and smug?

Do we draw others to God's Son during this most joyous time of the year or do we invite them to look elsewhere for the joy we so readily speak of but of which we show no evidence? God gives us joy, it is up to us whether we accept it and share it with all those we come in contact with or turn that joy into arrogance and keep it to ourselves seeing it as a reward for our "righteousness."

We are put in a position, as we await the celebration of the birth of Christ, that we can light up the lives of all who God brings to us this season, or be part and parcel of the thousand deaths that Christianity dies at the hands of believers who remain joyless in the presence of the radiant joy the Christ Child. That can be found nowhere else. Joy to the world...

DAILY READINGS:

Morning: Psalms 16: 7-11

I will praise the Lord, who counsels me; even at night my heart instructs me. I keep my eyes always on the Lord. With him at my right hand, I will not be shaken. Therefore my heart is glad and my tongue rejoices; my body also will rest secure, because you will not abandon me to the realm of the dead, nor will you let your faithful one see decay. You make known to me the path of life; you will fill me with joy in your presence, with eternal pleasures at your right hand.

Evening: I Peter 1: 6-9

In all this you greatly rejoice, though now for a little while you may have had to suffer grief in all kinds of trials. These have come so that your faith—of greater worth than gold, which perishes even though refined by fire—may be proved genuine and may result in praise, glory and honor when Jesus Christ is revealed.

Though you have not seen him, you love him; and even though you do not see him now, you believe in him and are filled with an inexpressible and glorious joy, for you are receiving the end result of your faith, the salvation of your souls.

DAY TWENTY-THREE

"All gold does not glitter; all who wander are not lost."

J.R.R. Tolkien

It seems that shiny things easily turn our heads. They don't have to be big, useful, or all that pretty, just as long as they shine. Shakespeare wrote "all that glitters is not gold," but we don't seem to care much, just as long as it glitters. It is difficult not to have our heads turned as we are bombarded by glitter everywhere we turn. Television, Internet, Blackberries and i-pads don't give us a moment's rest as our eyes continually sparkle with nothing but iron pyrite.

At Christmas time it seems to get even worse, the red, green, gold, and other bright colors, lights, and tinsel all speak of the glitter that catches our attention and serves only to distract us from the real gold we should seek beginning in Advent. While the world searches for anything that glitters, God is calling us to seek the gold that doesn't; the gold found in a hewed out, dirty stable some two thousand years ago. This gift given to mankind certainly did not glitter according to the world's standard, but is true gold beyond the greatest price; yet given to us at no cost.

Wandering and lost seem to be synonymous. Traveling aimlessly not sure what we are looking for, or even if we are looking for anything at all. But even in our wanderings, we may not be lost but wandering towards the one who calls us from the manger and the cross. We are only lost until we are found, and once found we may realize we were not lost, only wandering in the direction God had planned for us since the beginning of eternity.

As Christmas nears let us pray to see the true gold in our lives and in God's gift of His Son and wander towards the manger in Bethlehem.

DAILY READINGS:

Morning: Ezekiel 34:14-16

I will tend them in a good pasture, and the mountain heights of Israel will be their grazing land. There they will lie down in good grazing land, and there they will feed in a rich pasture on the mountains of Israel. I myself will tend my sheep and have them lie down, declares the Sovereign Lord. I will search for the lost and bring back the strays. I will bind up the injured and strengthen the weak, but the sleek and the strong I will destroy. I will shepherd the flock with justice.

Evening: I John 1: 5-7

This is the message we have heard from him and declare to you: God is light; in him there is no darkness at all. If we claim to have fellowship with him and yet walk in the darkness, we lie and do not live out the truth. But if we walk in the light, as he is in the light, we have fellowship with one another, and the blood of Jesus, his Son, purifies us from all sin.

DAY TWENTY-FOUR

"Forgiveness is the giving, and so the receiving, of life."

George MacDonald

Forgiveness can be a difficult thing. I don't think I have ever met anyone who was against the concept of forgiveness. That is, until they actually had something they had to forgive. In concept, forgiveness is a wonderful thing, yet in practice, it seems to be a bit difficult to swallow. Many times we would rather hold on to the hurt or injustice of the past than to forgive our transgressors and provide new life not only to those we need to forgive, but to ourselves as well.

The burden we carry by not forgiving is a cross that we need not bear. Forgiveness is not a feeling we must have before we actually do it, it is an act of our will and when we do forgive, we may readily find the feeling for which we have been searching. And it is in forgiving that we are forgiven.

In forgiveness we also give new life to something that had been broken and in doing so we receive new life as well. This Advent let us look to the one who came to us as a child not only to teach us to forgive, but to give his life so we could be forgiven.

DAILY READINGS:

Morning: Psalms 130:1-8

Out of the depths I cry to you, Lord; Lord, hear my voice. Let your ears be attentive to my cry for mercy. If you, Lord, kept a record of sins, Lord, who could stand? But with you there is forgiveness, so that we can, with reverence, serve you. I wait for the Lord, my whole being waits, and in his word I put my hope. I wait for the Lord more than watchmen wait for the morning, more than watchmen wait for the morning. Israel put your hope in the Lord, for with the Lord is unfailing love and with him is full redemption. He himself will redeem Israel from all their sins.

Evening: Acts 13:38-40

Therefore, my brothers and sisters, I want you to know that through Jesus the forgiveness of sins is proclaimed to you. Through him everyone who believes is set free from every sin, a justification you were not able to obtain under the Law of Moses. Take care that what the prophets have said does not happen to you.

DAY TWENTY-FIVE

"The Christian ideal has not been tried and found wanting; it has been found difficult and left untried."

G.K. Chesterton

True Christianity is not for the faint-hearted. It tests the very mettle of every man and woman who professes to believe. Life in this world has a way of beating everyone to their knees at one time or another, and believer or not, we all have to find a way to our feet and continue to carry on with what ever path we have chosen to travel.

To follow Jesus in this world provides us with challenges that nonbelievers tend not to have to face. With no faith to be tested or lost, one does not have to worry about their faith faltering. The question of seeing suffering in a world made by a God that is all good takes on a different and sometimes difficult question on why suffering happens for Christians compared to those who decide not to believe at all.

For us to live the life that God expects of us, loving our enemies, reaching out to the poor, turning the other cheek, not lying, stealing, or coveting, makes life far more difficult to live than not having those divine standards.

What God calls all of us to is not lacking but is the only path to a full and complete life. It is difficult because this world calls out for us to live the way we see fit.

Putting ourselves first and grabbing for all we can is easier than giving all we have to others. Is it no wonder that so many of us find it difficult and decide not to try it at all and by doing so miss the true joy of this life and the one that awaits us?

DAILY READINGS:

Morning: II Chronicles 19:11

Amariah the chief priest will be over you in any matter concerning the Lord, and Zebadiah son of Ishmael, the leader of the tribe of Judah, will be over you in any matter concerning the king, and the Levites will serve as officials before you. Act with courage, and may the Lord be with those who do well.

Evening: Philippians 1:20-21

I eagerly expect and hope that I will in no way be ashamed, but will have sufficient courage so that now as always Christ will be exalted in my body, whether by life or by death. For to me, to live is Christ and to die is gain.

DAY TWENTY-SIX

"Children are innocent and love justice, while most adults are wicked and prefer mercy."
G.K. Chesterton

Justice and mercy are not the same thing; they are two opposite sides of a coin that we all carry with us. One side is justice and we call for justice when we have been wronged. Someone must pay. We deserve retribution. We demand that someone make things right, even the score. Justify, justification — it is all the same. We have been offended, and things should be set right.

Mercy is the other side of the coin. It is what we ask for when we know we are guilty and are afraid of the justice we deserve. Justice is what we deserve; it is for mercy that we pray.

Justice is harsh; mercy is grace. Justice is measured; mercy is given freely. Justice is according to our merit; mercy is according to others. Justice is a process; mercy is immediate.

But if we ask for mercy as King David does so many times in the Psalms, we first have to admit that we need it. And by doing so we have to believe that we are indeed guilty. By being guilty, we deserve what we are due when we are wronged, but we ask for pardon.

God establishes both justice and mercy. If anyone is wronged by our transgressions and deserves to have a debt paid, it is He.

That raises the question: If we fall short of the standards that God has set for us, how do we face Him when He demands justice for our sins?

Just as God demands justice, He also provides the one thing that will satisfy our debt; His mercy. His divine mercy doesn't mean that our sins are excusable. If our offenses were acceptable, there would be no need for God's mercy. His forgiveness is not given because we deserve it, but because it is God's love to offer us the mercy we do not deserve instead of the justice He deserves.

It is during Advent that we should give thought to God's mercy as He sent Jesus as the personification of His forgiveness and the fulfillment of His promise of forgiveness. It is God saying "You have sinned and I demand justice just the same as you. You can't pay, but I will give you both justice and mercy in my Son. He will pay your debt. I love Him as I love you."

If we are willing to ask for God's mercy, we must be willing to be instruments of that same mercy to all those who God brings into our lives; to all who ask for our forgiveness as we ask for God's acceptance and His clemency.

DAILY READINGS:

Morning: Micah 6:8

He has shown all you people what is good. And what does the Lord require of you? To act justly and to love mercy and to walk humbly with your God.

Evening: James 2:12-13

Speak and act as those who are going to be judged by the law that gives freedom, because judgment without mercy will be shown to anyone who has not been merciful. Mercy triumphs over judgment.

DAY TWENTY-SEVEN

"I love you. I am at rest with you. I have come home."

> Dorothy L. Sayers

There is something about the word "home" that brings a peaceful feeling to most of us. The words house, residence, dwelling, abode, or domicile don't even come close. It doesn't matter whether you live in an eight-bedroom house or a one-bedroom apartment; it is home. A place that shelters us from the cold winds of this world, a place we can be at rest and find peace of mind and heart. It is a place like no other.

It is ironic that a child born in a stable and who had no place of His own to lay His head calls us home to His Father's house. "Come to me all you who are weary and heavy-laden and I will give you rest." Jesus gives our heart a home no matter how many roads we travel and how many empty fields we may cross. It is a home one begins in this world and continues throughout eternity.

As Advent comes to an end and we celebrate the birth of our Savior, there is no better time to be thankful and to embrace our home no matter where it is, small or large and all that make it a home. It is not the walls that make it a home - it is our family, friends, and all that brings joy and peace to our lives. It is the neighbor who waves to us in the morning, it is the person who delivers the mail and smiles and wishes us a good day, it is everyone we let into our lives and share the love God gave us. Let us come home.

DAILY READINGS:

Morning: Jeremiah 6:16

This is what the Lord says: "Stand at the crossroads and look; ask for the ancient paths, ask where the good way is, and walk in it, and you will find rest for your souls."

Evening: Luke 15:17-24

When he came to his senses, he said, "How many of my father's hired servants have food to spare, and here I am starving to death! I will set out and go back to my father and say to him: Father, I have sinned against heaven and against you. I am no longer worthy to be called your son; make me like one of your hired servants." So he got up and went to his father. But while he was still a long way off, his father saw him and was filled with compassion for him; he ran to his son, threw his arms around him and kissed him. The son said to him, "Father, I have sinned against heaven and against you. I am no longer worthy to be called your son." But the father said to his servants, "Quick! Bring the best robe and put it on him. Put a ring on his finger and sandals on his feet. Bring the fattened calf and kill it. Let's have a feast and celebrate. For this son of mine was dead and is alive again; he was lost and is found." So they began to celebrate.

DAY TWENTY-EIGHT

CHRISTMAS DAY

"The Son of God became a man to enable men to become the sons of God."

C.S. Lewis

Merry Christmas...

DAILY READINGS:

Luke 2:1-20

In those days Caesar Augustus issued a decree that a census should be taken of the entire Roman world. (This was the first census that took place while Quirinius was governor of Syria.) And everyone went to their own town to register.

So Joseph also went up from the town of Nazareth in Galilee to Judea, to Bethlehem the town of David, because he belonged to the house and line of David. He went there to register with Mary, who was pledged to be married to him and was expecting a child. While they were there, the time came for the baby to be born, and she gave birth to her firstborn, a son. She wrapped him in cloths and placed him in a manger, because there was no guest room available for them.

And there were shepherds living out in the fields nearby, keeping watch over their flocks at night. An angel of the Lord appeared to them, and the glory of the Lord shone around them, and they were terrified. But the angel said to them, "Do not be afraid. I bring you good news of great joy that will be for all the people. Today in the town of David a Savior has been born to you; he is the Messiah, the Lord. This will be a sign to you: You will find a baby wrapped in cloths and lying in a manger."

Suddenly a great company of the heavenly host appeared with the angel, praising God and saying, "Glory to God in the highest heaven, and on earth peace to those on whom his favor rests."

When the angels had left them and gone into heaven, the shepherds said to one another, "Let's go to Bethlehem and see this thing that has happened, which the Lord has told us about."

So they hurried off and found Mary and Joseph, and the baby, who was lying in the manger. When they had seen him, they spread the word concerning what had been told them about this child, and all who heard it were amazed at what the shepherds said to them. But Mary treasured up all these things and pondered them in her heart. The shepherds returned, glorifying and praising God for all the things they had heard and seen which were just as they had been told.

Chapter 5
DAILY READINGS FROM CHRISTMAS THROUGH EPIPHANY

Epiphany

In these current times it seems that Christmas begins far too early and ends far too soon. Many stores start to display Christmas ornaments, decorations, and gifts long before Thanksgiving, and many families have their Christmas tree by the curb shortly after Christmas dinner. I learned of Epiphany where I learned about most of the traditions and meaning of Christmas - from my grandparents.

Our tree was never taken down until after Epiphany when the celebration of the Christmas season formally ended. Epiphany is celebrated on January sixth, twelve days after Christmas, with the Sunday preceding January sixth celebrated as Epiphany Sunday.

Epiphany, which means to make known or to reveal, is the culmination of the Advent season and the twelve days of Christmas. As Advent anticipates the coming of the Christ Child, the twelve days after Christmas until Epiphany look to the coming of the Magi to worship the child who would become our Savior.

It is Interesting that the scriptures never speak of how many "Wise Men" actually came to see the baby Jesus or when they arrived. The Bible does mention the three gifts, gold, frankincense, and myrrh, but not how many men brought them.

Traditionally, Nativity scenes have the Kings from the East worshiping the newborn Savior along with the angels that heralded His birth and the shepherds that heard their news and rushed to the stable. Many scholars believe that the Magi arrived as much as two years later (citing King Herod's decree of killing all male children two years old and younger).

But no matter if or where tradition and lore intersect with factual history, the twelve days that lie between Christmas and Epiphany allow us to have the additional time to reflect on the miracle of Christmas and the coming of His revelation.

DAY ONE

"When you have found your own room, be kind to those who have chosen different doors and to those who are still in the hall."
C.S. Lewis

God calls each of us to Him in different ways. He alone knows what is in our heart of heart and the path that will lead us to Him and everlasting life. To some like St. Paul it took the vision of Jesus Himself to stop him in his tracks and to bring him to his knees. It was in this instance that a faith was born that would resound around the world and throughout the centuries.

God brought C.S. Lewis to his knees on a quiet ride in a motorcycle sidecar on his way to the zoo to a faith that also has resonated around the world and for all time to come. Both came to the same faith through different doors. But it is not difficult to see that both doors opened into the same room.

At times, I am surprised at how many of us who are Christians believe that the way that God called us to faith in Him is the only way. It is as if we think that we are more special than anyone else in His eyes and being so, any other path may not be genuine. Pride is at the heart of arrogance, even arrogance of our spirit.

There are many who have found other doors to belief in Christ. It doesn't matter if the door is large or small, wood or brass, red or green, all that matters is that we find the door prepared for us, open it and enter. And there still are many who are out in the hall searching for the door, and it is good to remember that they are as special in Jesus' eyes as we are. He is calling out to them and calling out to us to be kind to them as He is to us and was during our search.

As Christmas has passed and epiphany is before us, we would do well to recall that Mary and Joseph, the shepherds, and the wise men all came to the Christ Child through different doors.

DAILY READINGS:

Morning: Zechariah 7: 8-10

And the word of the Lord came again to Zechariah: This is what the Lord Almighty said: "Administer true justice; show mercy and compassion to one another. Do not oppress the widow or the fatherless, the foreigner or the poor. Do not plot evil against each other."

Evening: Acts 14: 26-27

From Attalia they sailed back to Antioch, where they had been committed to the grace of God for the work they had now completed. On arriving there, they gathered the church together and reported all that God had done through them and how he had opened a door of faith to the Gentiles.

DAY TWO

"It is our best work that God wants, not the dregs of our exhaustion. I think he must prefer quality to quantity."

George MacDonald

It is a lot easier to say we give God our best than to actually do so. There is so much in our daily lives with its countless distractions that our attention and energy are pulled into what seems like hundreds of different directions. Family, work, friends, and even church all call for our consideration and focus, leaving us with little to offer God but the dregs of our exhaustion.

It is our best that God asks of us. We owe Him the first fruits of our labors, not what we have left after we pay attention to everything else in our lives. If we claim that God has nothing but the best of our endeavors but give anything less, we give Him nothing at all. We expect the best that our Heavenly Father has to give and readily take it, and many times give little in return; fooling only ourselves if we think it is our best work that we lay before Him if it is not.

There is little doubt that the desire to give God nothing but our best work is deep in many of our hearts. The question is how can we turn these yearnings into action? The first step is knowing when we do and stop pretending when we don't. As with all things, we must go to God and tell Him that we know we are falling short and ask Him to rekindle the desire we once had to put God first.

God desires our honesty as much as the best we have to offer in all aspects of our lives. Anything less is foolish, worthless, and a waste of our time.

It may mean that we have to slow down and put some things away to see the real joy in our lives, the one we reflect upon at Christmas. The old saying that "less is more" is never truer than when we embrace less of the world and more of God.

DAILY READINGS:

Morning: Joshua 1:7-9

Be strong and very courageous. Be careful to obey all the law my servant Moses gave you; do not turn from it to the right or to the left, that you may be successful wherever you go. Keep this Book of the Law always on your lips; meditate on it day and night, so that you may be careful to do everything written in it. Then you will be prosperous and successful. Have I not commanded you? Be strong and courageous. Do not be afraid; do not be discouraged, for the Lord your God will be with you wherever you go.

Evening: Colossians 3:23-24

Whatever you do, work at it with all your heart, as working for the Lord, not for human masters, since you know that you will receive an inheritance from the Lord as a reward. It is the Lord Christ you are serving.

DAY THREE

"I want to encourage other people to try to discover who they are, not to try to fit into some superficial prototype of what they think a Christian should be, but to discover who they really are."

Larry Norman

We are all unique in God's eyes because we are all unique. God has created each of us in His own image and it is in His reflection that we are all different. Trying to be someone we are not or not called to be gets us nowhere fast, as God has set a path for each of us as singular as our personality, minds, and hearts.

In our lives we all encounter countless people who will try to tell us what God has planned for what we should be doing, who we should be, or us. It seems their advice is, more times than not, directed to make us more like them than who it is God wants us to become. There is nothing wrong with that except for the fact that we are not them. God created them to be who they are and as well meaning as they may be, they are trying to fit us in a preconceived mold of who it is that we should be.

Discovering who we are is a journey that may take us down a number of paths that may serve only to show us who we are not. Each turn that we take that proves to be the wrong one can help us eventually find the right one.

Even the wrong steps can bring us to the right place if we continually seek God and earnestly ask Him to lead and shape us into who He desires us to grow to be.

If we pray that God leads us to where He wants us to be and to show us who we really are, each step we take will eventually bring us to the knowledge of who we are and will take us home.

DAILY READINGS:

Morning: I Kings 18:20-21

So Ahab sent word throughout all Israel and assembled the prophets on Mount Carmel. Elijah went before the people and said, "How long will you waver between two opinions? If the Lord is God, follow him."

Evening: Romans 15:1-6

We who are strong ought to bear with the failings of the weak and not to please ourselves. We should all please our neighbors for their good, to build them up. For even Christ did not please himself but as it is written: "The insults of those who insult you have fallen on me." For everything that was written in the past was written to teach us, so that through the endurance taught in the Scriptures and the encouragement they provide we might have hope. May the God who gives endurance and encouragement give you the same attitude of mind toward each other that Christ Jesus had, so that with one mind and one voice you may glorify the God and Father of our Lord Jesus Christ.

DAY FOUR

"What do you call the man who wants to embrace the chimney sweep? A saint."

G. K. Chesterton

I have never met a chimney sweep or actually seen one in person. I am certain that there are not as many around as there used to be at the turn of the twentieth century. Pretty much all I know about them comes from my memories of Dick Van Dyke dancing atop the roofs in London along with a multitude of others at dusk in Mary Poppins. They seemed awfully happy and quite grimy.

We may not see many chimney sweeps any more, but we encounter their modern-day counterparts all the time. We see them on the street, in our offices, next to us in line at the grocery store and in front of us in the car pool line when we pick up our children from school. We see them in church from time to time as they come in the side or back door.

They are messy, may smell bad, and quite often are grungy. They embarrass us. The question is how do we react when we see them? Do we want to embrace them as Saint Francis, moved by compassion, embraced the leper on the road and finding in that simple act, God changed his heart and subsequently his life?

Or are we careful not to get too close, happy to share God's love with them...from afar. Do we turn away and act like we don't see them as they stand next to us? If they slide in the pew beside us do we all of a sudden see an "old friend" in another pew and hurry to worship beside them or quickly excuse ourselves telling our "chimney sweep friend" that we need to move closer to the front so we can hear better?

If Chesterton is right, and wanting to embrace the chimney sweep makes one a saint, what does ignoring them or trying to escape from their presence make us?

We all, as Christians, cherish our nativity scenes. The porcelain or plastic Christ Child so neat and clean makes us smile at the word that was made flesh. But being born in a stable was not like being born in the Bethlehem Regional Medical Center.

It was dirty, foul smelling, miserable, and the baby born in its midst most probably was too. But that didn't stop Mary, Joseph, and the shepherds from embracing the baby Jesus. We tell ourselves, if we had been there we would have done the same even though we refuse to embrace Jesus as He sits next to us in distressing disguise. We politely refuse to embrace Him as He reaches to embrace us whose sin and despair leaves us far worse in appearance than the worst chimney sweep imaginable.

DAILY READINGS:

Morning: 1 Samuel 2:7-8

The Lord sends poverty and wealth; he humbles and he exalts. He raises the poor from the dust and lifts the needy from the ash heap; he seats them with princes and has them inherit a throne of honor. For the foundations of the earth are the Lord's; on them he has set the world.

Evening: Acts 10:1- 4

At Caesarea there was a man named Cornelius, a centurion in what was known as the Italian Regiment. He and all his family were devout and God-fearing; he gave generously to those in need and prayed to God regularly. One day at about three in the afternoon he had a vision. He distinctly saw an angel of God, who came to him and said, "Cornelius!" Cornelius stared at him in fear. "What is it, Lord?" he asked. The angel answered, "Your prayers and gifts to the poor have come up as a memorial offering before God."

DAY FIVE

"I find that doing of the will of God leaves me no time for disputing about His plans."
George MacDonald

How do we know what God's will is? There is no shortage of people around that will quickly tell us what His will is for our lives, while many times acting like the one who sent the message instead of the one delivering it.

We all at times are susceptible to finding it easier to tell or at least think what God's will is for others rather than seriously seek it for ourselves. Fearing if we truly ask God to show us what His will is for us, He will actually show us and then we will have to decide if we will do it or not. That is fine if His will for us is what we want, but if it isn't, we have to either put aside our will in deference to His or follow our own will and pretend that it is His.

God shows us His will in every way imaginable, through His word, speaking to our heart, in the circumstances He surrounds us with, and in countless other ways. We have to continue to look and pray not only that God will show us His will, but also that we will recognize it as He reveals it to us.

We must also pray that we will accept it and follow it whether we like it or not. If one thing is certain, it is that God will not lead us to a place that we would not go ourselves, if we know where it would lead us in the beginning.

But when we do allow ourselves to see God's will in our lives and accept it, there is no greater peace and joy than finding it and reaching out to others in God's love. And by doing so, we find we have little time for arguing with the one who created us and only wants to fill our lives with the spirit that we have been searching for so long.

DAILY READINGS:

Morning: Deuteronomy 12: 28

Be careful to obey all these regulations I am giving you, so that it may always go well with you and your children after you, because you will be doing what is good and right in the eyes of the Lord your God.

Evening: John 14:23-27

Jesus replied, "Anyone who loves me will obey my teaching. My Father will love them, and we will come to them and make our home with them. Anyone who does not love me will not obey my teaching. These words you hear are not my own; they belong to the Father who sent me. All this I have spoken while still with you. But the Advocate, the Holy Spirit, whom the Father will send in my name, will teach you all things and will remind you of everything I have said to you. Peace I leave with you; my peace I give you. I do not give to you as the world gives. Do not let your hearts be troubled and do not be afraid.

DAY SIX

"If you look for truth, you may find comfort in the end; if you look for comfort you will not get either comfort or truth, only soft soap and wishful thinking to begin, and in the end, despair."

C.S. Lewis

I always thought it interesting that C.S. Lewis' autobiography was titled "Surprised by Joy." He chronicles his life and frames it within the context of his eventual search for truth. He did find the truth he was looking for but in doing so he found the comfort that Jesus spoke about in Matthew 12 where he told those who were listening to Him, "Come to me all you who are weary and heavy- laden and I will give you rest."

Lewis was not seeking comfort for his own sake. He was not looking to feel better or to be happy. He was looking for the eternal truth that only God can reveal. He discovered truth and found the comfort his soul needed in the bargain.

This leads me to believe that God knows the depths of our hearts and longings even if we aren't aware of them ourselves. Why wouldn't our creator know us better than we know ourselves? He knows whatever we think our desires are, as they all lead to our longing to know Him. Jesus said if we seek God's Kingdom first we find everything else we are looking for, whether we are aware of it or not.

If we seek truth for truth's sake we will find it and the comfort that we all long for and need so desperately. If we look for comfort for our own comfort's sake we will be searching for it our entire lives without success.

We may find it briefly in the distractions of the world we live in, only to find that we will be looking for it again and again.

We, like Lewis, will find comfort, only through the love of God, in finding truth. We will never find truth in trying to find comfort; in doing that we will find quickly that we will never receive either. That is, indeed, a circle that can only lead to despair.

DAILY READINGS:

Morning: Psalm 25:1-6

In you, Lord my God, I put my trust. I trust in you; do not let me be put to shame, nor let my enemies triumph over me. No one who hopes in you will ever be put to shame, but shame will come on those who are treacherous without cause. Show me your ways, Lord, teach me your paths. Guide me in your truth and teach me, for you are God my Savior, and my hope is in you all day long. Remember, Lord, your great mercy and love, for they are from of old.

Evening: John 14:1-7

Do not let your hearts be troubled. Trust in God; trust also in me. My Father's house has plenty of room; if that were not so, would I have told you that I am going there to prepare a place for you? And if I go and prepare a place for you, I will come back and take you to be with me that you also may be where I am. You know the way to the place where I am going." Thomas said to him, "Lord, we don't know where you are going, so how can we know the way?" Jesus answered, "I am the way and the truth and the life. No one comes to the Father except through me. If you really know me, you will know my Father as well. From now on, you do know him and have seen him."

DAY SEVEN

'Faithless is he that says farewell when the road darkens."

J.R.R. Tolkien

One of the easiest things we can do in our life in this world is to give up. When things become difficult, we become weary or frightened and it is simple for us to "throw in the towel." It is not just human nature that compels us to weaken during difficult times. Saint Peter found this out in the garden of Gethsemane when his spirit was willing but his flesh was weak. Tolkien points out that this weakening is a lack of our ability or willingness to look to our faith in God instead of ourselves.

As any road darkens before us it is easier to travel when we return to the light that only faith can shed. We have the ability in any difficult situation to choose to give up and say farewell and stumble through the darkness or call out in faith to the creator of light.

This season of Epiphany, it would serve us well to remember the Magi as they searched for the Christ Child through what history tells us may have been many years. Traveling far from their homes via the crudest form of travel, they must have encountered tremendous hardships. The road was well darkened but it was the Magi's faith that kept them from saying farewell to a journey that led them to Bethlehem and seeing the baby that would redeem mankind; a faith that was given light by a star that appeared in the East.

DAILY READINGS:

Morning: Psalms 59:16-17

But I will sing of your strength, in the morning I will sing of your love; for you are my fortress, my refuge in times of trouble. You are my strength, I sing praise to you; you, God, are my fortress, my God on whom I can rely.

Evening: John 16:31-33

"Do you now believe?" Jesus replied. "A time is coming and in fact has come when you will be scattered, each to your own home. You will leave me all alone. Yet I am not alone, for my Father is with me. I have told you these things, so that in me you may have peace. In this world you will have trouble. But take heart! I have overcome the world."

DAY EIGHT

"I would maintain that thanks are the highest form of thought, and that gratitude is happiness doubled by wonder."

G.K. Chesterton

Recently I wrote a note to my former high school principal thanking him for a kind gesture he did for me. I wanted him to know how much I appreciated his thoughtfulness and the fact that he took time to act on my behalf. I was surprised when he called me a few days later to thank me for sending him a thank-you note. I had to smile at the fact that he was thanking me for thanking him, and the thought that the sequence could have gone on forever (me thanking him for thanking me for thanking him and so on).

But as Chesterton states, the simple act of thanking someone transcends the deepest and most lofty thoughts that mankind has ever conceived. Most people I have met do not expect to be thanked for the good they do for others. They do good things because their hearts are kind and that is who they are. But I have not met anyone that I can recall whose feelings haven't been a bit bruised when thanks had not been offered by those close to them. If a thank you is the highest form of thought, then the absence of it has to be the lowest.

It is being thought of enough by someone else to receive their thanks that, at times, present a great wonder to us. How much more should we wonder at God's great gift of His Son at Christmastide?

A gift certainly beyond the greatest price that is given freely to all who will receive it. It is in the wonder of receiving this gift that we do not deserve that our eternal gratitude should echo continuously and be present in all our thoughts.

DAILY READINGS:

Morning: Isaiah 12: 4-6

In that day you will say: "Give praise to the Lord, call on his name; make known among the nations what he has done, and pro- claim that his name is exalted. Sing to the Lord, for he has done glorious things; let this be known to all the world. Shout aloud and sing for joy, people of Zion, for great is the Holy One of Israel among you."

Evening: Matthew 14:13-21

When Jesus heard what had happened, he withdrew by boat privately to a solitary place. Hearing of this, the crowds followed him on foot from the towns. When Jesus landed and saw a large crowd, he had compassion on them and healed their sick. As evening approached, the disciples came to him and said, "This is a remote place, and it's already getting late. Send the crowds away, so they can go to the villages and buy themselves some food."

Jesus replied, "They do not need to go away. You give them something to eat." "We have here only five loaves of bread and two fish," they answered. "Bring them here to me," he said. And he directed the people to sit down on the grass. Taking the five loaves and the two fish and looking up to heaven, he gave thanks and broke the loaves. Then he gave them to the disciples, and the disciples gave them to the people. They all ate and were satisfied, and the disciples picked up twelve basketfuls of broken pieces that were left over. The number of those who ate was about five thousand men, besides women and children.

DAY NINE

"Relying on God has to begin all over again every day as if nothing had yet been done..."
                                C.S. Lewis

At first this may sound strange, relying on God anew each day as if He had never done anything in our lives prior to our getting out of bed and as if we first met Him that morning. Does this mean that we should forget all that God has done in our lives and what we know He has done in the lives of others? I think, certainly not. David said in Psalms, "On my bed 1 remember you: I think of you through the watches of the night."

When Jesus taught the multitudes how to pray, He instructed them to ask Our Father to "give us this day our daily bread." Jesus didn't say that we should ask God for our monthly bread, weekly bread, or even a couple of days of bread; it is for our food and God's guidance that we should ask for each day. God doesn't let us store up His miracles or allow us to strengthen our faith by becoming complacent.

God gives us the faith, strength, and all we need to face each day, as each day dawns. If not, it would be very easy for us to forget the source of our power and think it comes from us instead of God. If we don't believe we have to ask each day, we may soon come to believe that we don't have to ask at all.

We can drive our car for years without thinking of maintenance, have no trouble and not think twice about whoever made it. But as soon as trouble starts, we waste no time in seeking a mechanic, wishing we had taken better daily care of our automobile. How much more are we apt to do the same with our faith?

Seeking God each day and relying on Him anew not only can help keep us from putting God on the shelf until we think we need Him, but opens the door for us to witness the wonderful gift of again seeing in amazement His wonders as if for the first time.

DAILY READINGS:

Morning: Lamentations 3:19-26

I remember my affliction and my wandering, the bitterness and the gall. I well remember them, and my soul is downcast within me. Yet this I call to mind and therefore I have hope: Because of the Lord's great love we are not consumed, for his compassions never fail. They are new every morning; great is your faithfulness. I say to myself, "The Lord is my portion; therefore I will wait for him." The Lord is good to those whose hope is in him, to the one who seeks him; it is good to wait quietly for the salvation of the Lord.

Evening: Luke 11:1-4

One day Jesus was praying in a certain place. When he finished, one of his disciples said to him, "Lord, teach us to pray, just as John taught his disciples." He said to them, "When you pray, say: 'Father, hallowed be your name, your kingdom come. Give us each day our daily bread. Forgive us our sins, for we also forgive everyone who sins against us. And lead us not into temptation."

DAY TEN

"Men feel that cruelty to the poor is a kind of cruelty to animals. They never feel that it is an injustice to equals; nay it is treachery to comrades."
                                        G.K. Chesterton

I don't know where the division between rich and poor began. I am not talking about the difference in financial means, but in the attitude that many of us have in how we may look at those who are less fortunate. It is easy to look upon them with pity as we do at a lost dog we get a glimpse of as we are driving down the highway. We feel sorry for them and their plight, and may try to reach out to them, but not necessarily as an equal, but as any compassionate person may do to a hungry kitten.

If we see a news report, read of a landlord evicting a family who can not pay their rent, or read about a single mother who is working three jobs but still can't afford to feed or clothe her children, we feel a twinge of sympathy and may even try to find them and offer help. But do we reach out to them because we see a brother or sister in a time of trouble or do we just toss them a bone thinking we have done a good deed for someone who we view consciously or unconsciously who may be lesser than ourselves?

Not seeing all men as equal only diminishes who we are, not those we see as less significant. And if all we feel is sympathy for those less fortunate, we lower them in our eyes to that of a mistreated animal. It is when we realize that we share the same Father that any injustice to them is an act of treason. Those being wronged should anger us as we see a comrade or a friend, being treated in a way we would not stand for, if it were us who were being treated unkindly.

The Magi traveled across the known world to worship a child born to a poor couple who were sent to sleep with the cows.

They didn't look upon them as lower them themselves, but knelt in awe at the baby wrapped in rags who although was above us all, came to serve.

DAILY READINGS:

Morning: Psalms 9:7-10

The Lord reigns forever; he has established his throne for judgment. He rules the world in righteousness and judges the peoples with equity. The Lord is a refuge for the oppressed, a stronghold in times of trouble. Those who know your name trust in you, for you Lord, have never forsaken those who seek you.

Evening: Luke 11:39-46

Then the Lord said to him, "Now then, you Pharisees clean the outside of the cup and dish, but inside you are full of greed and wickedness. You foolish people! Did not the one who made the outside make the inside also? But now as for what is inside you—be generous to the poor, and everything will be clean for you. Woe to you Pharisees, because you give God a tenth of your mint, rue and all other kinds of garden herbs, but you neglect justice and the love of God. You should have practiced the latter without leaving the former undone. Woe to you Pharisees, because you love the most important seats in the synagogues and respectful greetings in the marketplaces. Woe to you, because you are like unmarked graves, which people walk over without knowing it." One of the experts in the law answered him, "Teacher, when you say these things, you insult us also." Jesus replied, "And you experts in the law, woe to you, because you load people down with burdens they can hardly carry, and you yourselves will not lift one finger to help them."

DAY ELEVEN

"One can only choose a side. So I now choose my side. I choose beauty; I choose what I love. But choosing to believe is believing. It's all I can do: choose. I confess my doubts and ask my Lord Christ to enter my life. I do not know God is, I do but say; be it done to me according to my will."

Sheldon Vanauken

We all choose sides whether we are aware of it or not. Even not choosing a side is actually choosing, as we will be on the side of those who will not decide. We have all heard it said that life is full of choices. Every day we decide when we are going to get up, what we will eat, what we are going to wear, and dozens of other things that we take for granted and choose without much thought. And in the overall scheme of things, most of those daily choices don't end up mattering much.

I had heard somewhere that the word 'decide' comes from a Greek word that means "to cut off"; meaning that once we decide or choose something we cut off all other available options. If we look at a menu and decide on the chicken salad we cut off everything else the bill of fare offers. Each choice we make cuts off everything else we may be considering.

Certainly many choices we make do matter, if and who we marry, if we have children, and what vocation we will follow are just a few of countless choices we make that have an effect that resounds throughout our lives.

But there is one choice that we all have to make that is above all, and that is the choice that Vanauken wrote about in his first book "A Severe Mercy," the choice of choosing God or not.

Jesus asked probably the most important question ever asked, "Who do you say that I am?"

A question that each one of us has to answer and a question that echoes throughout the ages. Mary had to choose in the presence of the angel Gabriel, Joseph had to choose after God spoke to him in a dream, and King Herod had to choose after questioning the Magi.

This is where the center of the ages touches down and reaches our heart. As Vanauken admitted, just the act of choosing to believe is the crux of believing itself. Faith is not a feeling; it is an act of our will. It is in that moment of choosing God, even in the midst of doubts, that our fears can only melt away and that Christ Jesus enters our lives. The choice is ours.

DAILY READINGS:

Morning: Deuteronomy 30:11-19

Now what I am commanding you today is not too difficult for you or beyond your reach. It is not up in heaven, so that you have to ask, "Who will ascend into heaven to get it and proclaim it to us so we may obey it?" Nor is it beyond the sea, so that you have to ask, "Who will cross the sea to get it and proclaim it to us so we may obey it?"

No, the word is very near you; it is in your mouth and in your heart so you may obey it. See, I set before you today life and prosperity, death and destruction. For I command you today to love the Lord your God, to walk in obedience to him, and to keep his commands, decrees and laws; then you will live and increase, and the Lord your God will bless you in the land you are entering to possess. But if your heart turns away and you are not obedient, and if you are drawn away to bow down to other gods and worship them, I declare to you this day that you will certainly be destroyed. You will not live long in the land you are crossing the Jordan to enter and possess. This day I call the heavens and the earth as witnesses against you that I have set before you life and death, blessings and curses. Now choose life, so that you and your children may live and that you may love the Lord your God, listen to his voice, and hold fast to him. For the Lord is your life, and he will give you many years in the land he swore to give to your fathers, Abraham, Isaac and Jacob.

Evening: Romans 15:13

May the God of hope fill you with all joy and peace, as you trust in him, so that you may overflow with hope by the power of the Holy Spirit.

DAY TWELVE

EPIPHANY

"I believe in Christianity as I believe that the sun has risen: not only because I see it, but because by it I see everything else."

C.S. Lewis

We do not have to actually see the sun to know it is there. Its brightness illuminates everything on which it shines. The light it gives makes it easy for us to see all that is around, keeps us from stumbling, and gives us a much better perspective of the world. Its absence tends to skew our perception on just about everything. It is in dim light and darkness that we can easily lose our way.

Without the sun, we can only view things through fog or darkness. That makes all we encounter look different. A road that may look safe to us in our sight that is limited by the dark may actually be the precipice that could easily endanger us or end our life. By the light of the sun we see things as they really are. The higher the sun the less the shadows, which is more of the sun that is exposed, the better we see. And the better we see the safer we are.

Christianity, as Lewis discovered, is the same as the sun. It gives a light to our lives that no other faith can claim. When Jesus said at the temple, "I am the light of the world; whoever follows me will never walk in darkness," He spoke of what Lewis wrote. Jesus also said that a moment before he spat on the ground and put the mud on the eyes of the blind man and gave him his sight.

This is also of what Lewis wrote. What He told the crowd in the temple, many might consider a metaphor, what He told the blind man was as stark as the truth could be.

Thanks to the love of Jesus, the blind man who could finally see did not only see everything for the first time by the sun, but I am sure he saw everything differently because of God's Son.

Now that Christmastide has ended for another year and a new year is still in its infancy, there is no better time to pray that the light of Christianity will shine brightly in our lives this year. Let us pray that we will see every day, every situation, opportunity, or person we meet by the light of our faith, and that light and faith will move us closer to God's love and reaching out to others.

DAILY READINGS:

Morning: Isaiah 60:19-20

The sun will no more be your light by day, nor will the brightness of the moon shine on you, for the Lord will be your everlasting light, and your God will be your glory. Your sun will never set again, and your moon will wane no more; the Lord will be your everlasting light, and your days of sorrow will end.

Evening: 1 John 1:5-7

This is the message we have heard from him and declare to you: God is light; in him there is no darkness at all. If we claim to have fellowship with him and yet walk in the darkness, we lie and do not live out the truth. But if we walk in the light, as he is in the light, we have fellowship with one another, and the blood of Jesus, his Son, purifies us from all sin

ABOUT THE AUTHOR

William Murdock began studying the works of C.S. Lewis shortly after becoming a Christian his senior year in high school. Raised as a Catholic, he returned to the faith of his youth after a number of years of studying the works of Lewis, G.K. Chesterton, George MacDonald, J.R.R. Tolkien, Sheldon Vanauken, Joy Davidman, Dorothy Sayers, Charles Williams, and Thomas Merton.

Educated at Asheville-Buncombe Technical Community College, Mars Hill College, Duke University, Harvard University, and Stanford University, he is the founding director of the Eblen Charities and the Eblen Center for Social Enterprise in Asheville, North Carolina. Murdock has taught for the Duke University Nonprofit Management Program and has taught courses on C.S. Lewis and the Chronicles of Narnia at the University of North Carolina at Asheville. He has written for the Duke University Program, local and national publications, and has authored several biographies.